A New World
in the Morning

The Biopsychological Revolution

A NEW WORLD IN THE MORNING

The Biopsychological Revolution

by DAVID P. YOUNG

THE WESTMINSTER PRESS
Philadelphia

ISBN 0-664-24949-3

Library of Congress Catalog Card No. 77-183590

158.1
yo8N
93047
april 1975

BOOK DESIGN BY
DOROTHY ALDEN SMITH

Published by The Westminster Press ®
Philadelphia, Pennsylvania

PRINTED IN THE UNITED STATES OF AMERICA

To the "Long Shadow of a Tall Man"
                                        —E. Fay Campbell

A giant of a man who has spent his life in love with the world and all of God's creation.

To my children's children

Their world will be so different from ours, but if they love it, meaning in being human will be found.

Contents

Preface

It is a humbling experience to sit down and think about the endless numbers of persons who have challenged your mind with their humanness and creativity. I hope that this book will repay that challenge in some significant measure. I would like to write a paragraph about each person who has helped by reading the draft manuscript, but space will only allow a paragraph of their names to stand as my official record of appreciation for their sharing of time and insights. These people can be credited with a major role in what has survived as good in the book. I, alone, am responsible for its faults and the inability to hear their suggestions clearly.

My thanks to Maryvillians: Esther Swenson, mind picker and challenger par excellence whose depth of understanding is fantastic and exciting to confront; Paul Ogren, chemical cohort who continually probes and pushes for excellence in all areas of humanness; Dorothy Murphree, author and playwright with overflowing creativity and zest; and Bill Hutton, chemistry graduate student with a rare combination of concern for chemistry and for people. And to others: Edna Young, my aunt and a person whose sensitivity has always been guided by joy and meaning; Nancy Nichols, a close friend from college days who combines love and life in a beautiful way; Betty Warren, tutor/searcher/friend to all—if only her kind would multiply, what a wonderful world we would live in; and Mark Davis, my old jogging buddy who continually jogs mind and life with wit, whim, and wisdom.

Typing thanks go to Dona White, Judy Davis, and Marilyn Howell, three of a bevy of vivacious, smiling secretaries at Cornell University; to Sweet Young, my wife, and what more can I say than "I love you!"; and last but not least, to "my favorite typist," Margie Ross, whose smile for life never vanishes.

It is always difficult to pin down exact beginnings, but this particular effort got its starting impetus when Roland W. Tapp wrote to me in response to an article I had written on cloning. Good fortune resulted in his eventually becoming a helpful guide as my editor. The actual writing was done during the last half of a sabbatical leave taken at Cornell University. A National Science Foundation Science Faculty Fellowship made it possible for me to spend the 1970–1971 academic year with the Cornell Program on Science, Technology and Society. The warm atmosphere provided there by Franklin A. Long, Raymond Bowers, and Robert S. Morison created the nourishment and encouragement for me to proceed seriously into the interdisciplinary area of the impact and interplay between science and society. Gentlemen, thank you.

Many group situations have also provided a training ground for ideas presented in this book. Important ones have been the science faculty at Maryville College, the persevering Maryville students who have struggled creatively with "different" science courses, the "heads" in a mind control course at Cornell, and study groups at New Providence Presbyterian Church in Maryville, Tennessee, and the First Presbyterian Church in Ithaca, New York.

So, gang, thanks for being you. I hope that in my being me, we will all find more meaning in life and in our contact with fellow men and women.

D. P. Y.

Maryville College

Our modern world
was created in less than
ten thousand years, and
in the last two hundred
years it has changed faster
than in all the previous
millennia.

Something is happening
in the structure of
human consciousness.
It is another species
of life that is just
beginning.

Pierre
Teilhard
de
Chardin

No evolutionary
future awaits man
except in
association with
all other men.

The future
of the earth is in
our hands.
How shall we decide?

Prologue:
To Build the Earth

Picking up a book without an introduction or preface frustrates me. I am always curious as to what the author is hoping to accomplish. So now that I am getting my shot at the author's game, I feel compelled to begin by explaining some of the mood and dialogue I hope to generate. It is never easy to condense one's thought and feeling into a few sentences; however, a few lines written by Teilhard de Chardin come very close to doing this for me: "Something is happening in the structure of human consciousness. It is another species of life that is just beginning." [1]

Ever since evolutionary direction produced the creature we call man, he has been continually developing and changing. Man has never been a static creature, but it is my thesis that we are currently witnessing and participating in some changes that will result in man emerging as a new "species of life." Still man, to be sure, but yet, a New Man.

Today much attention and energy is being focused on the mélange of problems covered by the umbrella terms of ecology and environment. This is good and necessary, and indeed I hope that in some way I can contribute to the solution of these problems in my role both as a citizen and as a college professor. But as important as the eco-issue is, my book is centered around the concern of what I shall call the rapidly approaching biopsychological revolution. (The word "biopsychological" is used in a general sense. "Bio" refers to man as a living organism, how he functions, and how he reproduces. "Psychological" refers to the mind of man and what he thinks of himself, his fellowmen, and his place in the universe.) Although it will not happen overnight or without tremendous effort and cost, I have the optimism that we will solve our population and pollution problems. In fact, we had better solve them, for inherent in the solution of these eco-problems is the assurance of our continued survival as a species. But on the other hand, I am also concerned that we may in effect be "saving" ourselves for jumping from the frying pan into the fire. Perhaps this metaphor is a bit strong, but the point is that at the same time we devote great energies and expense in cleaning up our environment, we are also edging closer and closer to a biopsychological revolution that will not so much threaten species survival, as does the eco-problem, but rather threaten species identity. In other words, man is now in possession of enough scientific knowledge to become the first species in the three billion years of evolutionary history to attempt to change itself by deliberate and purposeful experimentation. Man is preparing in a new way to program his own future rather than to continue to flow along with the currents of natural selection. In short, man is now ready to experiment on man. Man will change man.

The purpose of this book, then, is to look at some areas of modern science that in a very important sense threaten the very way in which life has operated for Homo sapiens since he first appeared on the evolutionary scene some thirty-five thousand years ago. No attempt will be made at predicting a Biopsychological Doomsday. In fact, it is hoped that a feeling will be created that these changes confronting us contain within themselves a fantastic possibility for a future that is not only positive and good (admittedly, two difficult terms to define), but that will have the potential to produce a greater fulfillment of life than ever before possible. Certainly such advances will not come automatically. Man is just as capable of fumbling the biopsychological ball as he is now fumbling the eco-ball. (Let's hope that he doesn't drop either one!) The crucial dilemma facing man is how he will choose and whether or not he will lose his "nerve" in the face of the stakes at hand—species identity.

If I knew the answers to the questions that will be raised by the writing to follow, then there would have been no need for the book. Indeed, that is where we are at this moment in time—trying to define the proper questions so that we can dialogue and debate on the important issues, options, and solutions. There will be no simple or obvious answers. Man is already too complex a creature for that. But even knowing that there will be many different points of view does not lessen the burden of finding answers for the future. Questions are important, but an additional hope of mine is that the framework of asking them in this book will create self-motivation on the part of the reader to seek out additional information on what he comes to conceive as the crucial or pivotal points.

To sum up why I have written this book, I would say that it stems from my view that man today is not yet what he can be or what he was meant to be. In other words, there are new levels of creativity and being for man to climb to, and it is entirely possible that in order for him to reach those levels, he is going to have to enter into experimental alteration and contact with himself as a species. Yet in the coming biopsychological revolution I can see both threat and promise. The threat lies in the possibility of creating even more subtle and powerful methods for one man to control another than we have now. On the other side of the coin, the promise, lies the opportunity to generate new levels of expression of the joy and meaning of life by removing some of the debilitating aspects of mind and reproduction. My own view of things is that I would much rather confront the promise than the threat, although unfortunately neither one can be ignored or treated separately.

ORGANIZATION
OF THE BOOK

The opening chapter, "On Our Way to the Future, Science Is Changing the Rules of the Game," is an attempt to show that the future will not be like yesterday. But the kinds of changes I am talking about in the future are not smogless automobiles magnetically driven at speeds of two hundred miles per hour but rather radical changes in the nature of the rules whereby we play the game of life. Specifically, these changes are described in terms of the ways in which we beget children and use our brains.

To illustrate this contention concerning the rules of the game, three areas of science will be discussed in Chapters 2 through 7. The first area of mood drugs is one that has been with us since the beginning of history. However, it has begun to weave its way into Western culture in a new way beginning with the decade of the 1960's. The second area of electrical stimulation of the brain deals with scientific knowledge that has only recently become a part of the arena of human experimentation. The last area, that of sexual reproduction, deals with knowledge that is being generated in the animal and plant worlds but that has not yet been applied to humans. (Maybe!) Thus Chapters 2 through 7 should be treated as three pairs of two. The first chapter of each pair (2, 4, and 6) is designed to provide a short lesson in the fundamental science or possibilities in each area. The second chapter of each pair (3, 5, and 7) has been written with a view toward providing a meaningful framework for discussion and dialogue on the critical or pivotal issues involved in each area. To do this, these latter chapters have been divided into four parts: (1) an opening preamble written from my point of view but with an attempt to create a somewhat different than usual perspective as a jumping-off point for discussion, (2) a listing of reasons to favor or oppose further developments, (3) quotations from various authors to serve as views for reflection, and (4) questions and short statements or situations designed to serve as focal points for people with differing views to get into communication with each other. If, in your efforts, you design or come across additional pro or con views, quotations, or questions, I would very much hope that you will take the time and effort to write me about them. Your feedback might help put me on the right track.

The concluding chapter, "A New World in the Morning," is a personal viewpoint focused on some basic points concerning not only the options that face us but also the call to a new life-style which I feel must develop if we are to meet the future that awaits us. Although it is in part giving away the ending, I would like to say here that in my view we can't stop now. Man is just too inquisitive a character to call a halt to the seeking or application of knowledge. But on the other hand, I agree with the ethicist Paul Ramsey that there may be some things we can do, that we should not do. I wish we could say that now, for example, about the dropping of the atomic bombs on Japan in World War II. But I don't want to end this prologue on a pessimistic or backward-looking note, so I will turn again to Teilhard de Chardin for a provocative and very beautiful statement: "The task before us now, if we would not perish, is to shake off our ancient prejudices, and to build the earth." [2]

It is preposterous to assume that my book will help build the earth, but I would be less than honest if I didn't say that I truly hope that somehow it will create a "brick" of action in our lives that will help to do just that: "shake off our ancient prejudices" and "build the earth."

1

On Our Way to the Future, Science Is Changing the Rules of the Game

Do you remember the first verse of the poem "Jabberwocky" that Alice encountered in her trip Through the Looking-Glass?

> Twas brillig, and the slithy toves
>   Did gyre and gimble in the wabe;
> All mimsy were the borogoves,
>   And the mome raths outgrabe.

In a very real sense this poem represents the way in which the realm of science * has drifted into a world of specialization and jargon which for the most part has lost communication with the everyday world of the proverbial man in the street. Indeed, our past history shows

---

* Although in some discussions it is worthwhile to distinguish between science and technology, I have chosen to use only the word "science." From a simple point of view, one can say that technology deals with the practical applications of the ideas generated by a science that is itself interested only in discovery for the sake of discovery. However, in our modern world they both feed each other by the process of mutually raising questions and possibilities to consider. Therefore, it seems to me that for general purposes they have fused together to produce a synergistic complex of ideas and action which contribute to the new levels of change we are experiencing.

that we have long been on a kind of Dr. Jekyll-Mr. Hyde seesaw swinging back and forth from meaningful contact to distance between the nonscientist and the scientist. But in our age the balance has surely shifted in the direction of science so that it is again time to narrow the gap and renew the bond between science and society. In short, science is no longer speaking a language that society can understand. To illustrate, let us turn to an encounter between Linus and Lucy in the Peanuts world created by Charles Schulz.

That precisely is the problem: how to speak a language that all men can understand, or how to begin to communicate in a way so that the quality and meaning of life can be enhanced instead of continually having to face the prospect of being "slugged" (whether by the sphere of science, politics, or religion). To survive in the future world will require a new level of understanding, which is to say that the underlying assumption of this whole issue is that we must bridge the many communication gaps that exist. My particular bias, then, leads me to suggest that before we can consider some of the details of current science and the impact they might have on the creature man, we must say a few words about four things: (1) the future, (2) the game called science, (3) the new rules of the game, and (4) the interface between science and society. Attaining this perspective is a prerequisite for attempts to bridge the communication gap.

From *Peanuts* ®, by Charles M. Schulz
© 1957 United Feature Syndicate, Inc.

The Future
Will Not Resemble the Past

Tomorrow will not be like yesterday. That is a statement on which I am sure we could all readily agree. Although we often live as if it were not so, change is really the only constant of man's existence. Nevertheless, we are now standing on a threshold of change that is genuinely of another dimension and scope from that of our past.

Let me illustrate in two ways. First, in looking into our past, we have learned that it once took the precursor of modern man a million years to change from a creature using pebble tools to one using a chipped stone ax held in the hand. However, in our present world, the Wright brothers began the century by reaching one of man's long dreamed of goals—flight. In 1904 they shattered the shackles of gravity with a flight in a heavier-than-air machine that flew what is now the absurd distance of 120 feet. But think for a moment. It has taken man only a span of sixty-five years, one average lifetime, literally to jump from the sand dunes of Kitty Hawk, North Carolina, to the dusty craters of Tranquillity Base, Moon. It once took man a million years to discover a new hand tool, but we are now standing on a pyramid of knowledge such that the time span between learning how to fly and leaving the planet is measured by the handful of three score and five years.

A second way of viewing this accelerated rate of change and the relationship between the future and the past has been suggested by Alvin Toffler in his book *Future Shock*. Homo sapiens, modern man, appears to have arrived on the evolutionary continuum somewhere around 35 to 50 thousand years ago. Toffler suggests that if we were to take the last 50,000 years of man's existence and divide them into 800 lifetimes of 62 years each, we would note that "only during the last six lifetimes did masses of men ever see a printed word" and "only in the last two has anyone anywhere used an electric motor." [1] Indeed, when one makes even a short list of some of the achievements that have arrived in this last lifetime—worldwide instantaneous communication of sound and picture, routine air travel near the speed of sound, and heart transplants—one gets a vivid reminder of the accelerated pace of change that we have come to accept as a part of life. This kind of accelerated change creates a new pressure of choice, for in the face of such rapid movement man must turn his face toward the future in a new way, or that future, when it arrives, just might not be the kind that he likes or had in mind.

Looking for a moment into the crystal ball, I think we can have some fun conjuring up newspaper headlines that may seem ridiculous to us now, but which very well may be page 34 news tomorrow.

AUTO ACCIDENT KILLS 8
BUT DOCTORS FIND ENOUGH PARTS
TO PRODUCE 3 NEW PEOPLE

Jury to Debate on Which Names
Should Be Used

WEDDING STOPPED

Bride Exposed as Part Human—Part Machine

HOUSEWIFE RECEIVES SECOND BRAIN
TRANSPLANT

Didn't Like Being a Scientist, So Returns
to First Life as Belly Dancer

NEW PILL CAUSES REVERSAL IN SEX

LATEST FAD IN FAMILY LIFE
IS FOR HUSBAND AND WIFE TO CHANGE SEX

He Becomes She and She Becomes He

SPECIAL: CHARLIE'S BABY BARGAIN BASEMENT

Clearance of Blue-Eyed Blond Girl Embryos—
Guaranteed to Grow to Minimum of 40–23–38

*JIM RYUN RUNS TWO-MINUTE MILE
WITH AID OF SECOND HEART*

PRESIDENT FROZEN
TO BE AWAKENED IN 22D CENTURY

*Maybe the War in Vietnam Will Be Over Then,
Says President, Seconds Before Freezing*

From the outset let it be understood that this is not an
attempt to predict what awaits us in the future. Even
Edison, with all his creative genius, has been reported to
have remarked in 1889: "I have always consistently op-

posed high-tension and alternating systems of electric lighting . . . not only on account of danger but because of their general unreliability and unsuitability for any general systems of distribution." [2] Recent blackouts and brownouts notwithstanding, within a lifetime of that statement the United States was literally enveloped with an electrical spider web which provided not only lighting but power to open cans, sharpen pencils, and grind garbage.

In the past century we have experienced some unprecedented changes in our physical environment so that we now spend most of our time in man-made cubicles in which all the basic elements of comfort are at our fingertip control—heat, cold, water, food, and light, not to mention the multitude of devices for sound communication that we use nearly every waking moment. Yet, in many ways, we are becoming saturated with physical change, for what else is there left to heat or air-condition? The kind of future I have in mind is one that does not concern our physical environment but is rather one in which we will attempt to program changes in our biological and psychological nature—in ourselves as human beings.

The thresholds we are now contemplating crossing are in some sense as profound in their drastic nature and far-reaching implications as the long past evolutionary changes that occurred when the first self-replicating molecules were formed or when life first crawled out of the frothing seas onto dry land. In a very real sense I think that man's knowledge of science is moving him toward the next "big" step in evolution. It may be the height of arrogance or stupidity, but man's science is preparing to challenge Mother Nature on her own terms. John Platt, a noted biophysicist, has put it most bluntly: "This generation marks the time when evolution by natural selection is replaced by evolution by human selection." [3] But let there be no misunderstanding—if man wrests control of nature from Mother Nature herself, this will not come free, there will be some kind of cost to pay or response to reckon with. Man represents only one species among millions woven into an intricate organization of mutual interdependence. Any change that man makes or action that he takes inevitably has an impact on the rest of nature. A simple but well-known example is the fact that indiscriminate spraying of DDT to get rid of the Dutch elm disease results in a robinless silent spring.

Said in a different way, we are asking scientific questions today that not only were inconceivable a few centuries ago, but which if asked would have been totally impossible to answer at that time. But as I hope the next six chapters will show, there can be no doubt about the fact that man is now making experimental choices about his biological and psychological destiny which will challenge the natural selection pressure of timeless Mother Nature. Surely it is impossible to judge now the possible impact of such decisions, but clearly we know enough already to realize that our bullish assault on insects and bacteria with pesticides and antibiotics in the past few decades has altered considerably those two vast worlds of life. Our future horizon is one that has the potential of changing drastically what it means to be a human—to be a person—to be a man or a woman. We are preparing to challenge Mother Nature in a way so as to add a totally new dimension to the ancient query of the writer of the Eighth Psalm:

> When I look at thy heavens, the work of
>   thy fingers,
>   the moon and the stars which thou
>   hast established;
> what is man that thou art mindful of
>   him?

(Ps. 8:3–4a.)

What is man? It is the thesis of this book that this question is going to have a new answer, not by the chance of natural selection, but by man's own deliberate design and choice.

At the risk of beating to death this point about the future, I would like to interject two additional comments concerning the fact that the gaining of knowledge carries with it, as the other side of the coin, the necessity of dealing with its uses and implications. So two quick points: first, planning and second, guidance. The futurist Robert Theobald has sharpened the issue of planning with the following statement: "Almost all of our study, our planning, our actions, continue to be based on the assumption that the future will resemble the past." [4] He is right in his implication. This kind of assumption is just no longer viable. We know that the world is getting more and more complex every day, but the true impact of this fact is deceptively hidden by the ease with which we make phone calls from our private instrument to any one of millions like it all over the planet, or do something as simple as switch on the lights or turn a handle to get a drink of water. But close your eyes for a moment and try to imagine the maze of wires and piping that exists to make this possible. If you try to follow them all, you will never open your eyes again.

Another element in this complexity of planning is the vast amount of information that is flowing through our society. With the mass of knowledge in some areas doubling every ten years, someday soon it will be possible for scientists to keep up-to-date using traditional methods only in an increasingly smaller area, say, for example, tropical diseases of the left toes of righthanded bald barbers. It seems to me obvious that in a world with so many physical accessories for life and a burgeoning information base, it is ridiculous to think that tomorrow's problems will require the same kind of planning and methods as those needed ten or one hundred years ago. And nothing has been said here about the problems of the gap between those who have and those who have not. If we plan for this eventuality as we did before, then we are in for some rocky times.

The second point is guidance. Where do we turn for direction in our plunge into the future? Margaret Mead has argued that in the West we are now entering a culture in which one's peers, rather than one's parents, emerge as the model for behavior. In the past there were always some elders who knew more than the youngsters what life, growing up, and experience were all about. Not so today. There are just no elder authorities to turn to who have grown up in a culture with satellites, trips to the moon, heart transplants, instantaneous worldwide communication of wars and sporting events, and computerized credit. Or stated in another way, Mead writes that we are moving "into a present for which none of us was prepared by our understanding of the past." [5] To be sure, we are facing some gigantic problems—even a new word has been coined to express them collectively: popollution, a condensation of population and pollution.[6] But we must face up to the fact that no adult can invoke his youth on us in order to convince us of the correct path to take. This does not mean turning the world over to those under thirty. It does mean, however, that past prejudices and attitudes are going to have to be as critically examined as those of the new consciousness or counter-culture.

To put it more bluntly, the institutions of our past— science, religion, politics, etc.—just do not provide a framework of guidance that will allow us to plan appropriately for the future. This does not mean we should ignore the past. We need to study it and learn from it, but we are faced with the prospect of creating radically new frameworks for planning and guidance. As Robert Heinlein, one of the deans of science fiction writing, puts it: "Whatever you do, *do not let the past be a straitjacket!*" [7]

THE GAME
CALLED SCIENCE

It seems to me that one of the key factors in the poor communication surrounding science is that many people (including some scientists) do not have an adequate understanding of the framework of scientific inquiry. It is a caricature to be sure, but a great deal of science education and teaching has been concerned with the memorization of the names of the trees, with very little effort or thought being put into discovering the pathways between the trees or the nature of the forest itself. Until one can see beyond the popular shibboleths of total objectivity, inherent truthfulness, and irrefutability of facts in science, one will not be in any position to ask proper questions about where scientific knowledge can take man.

Let us get into this subject by asking why it has taken man so long to reach the point where he is today. Although the ideas of force, energy, and mass had been kicked around in some form for three thousand years, it never seriously occurred to man until Galileo and Newton that they could be formulated and discussed in such a manner as to be able to manipulate them in a predictable way. But what does it mean to be scientific? How is a scientific man different from a nonscientific man? Very simply, but very crucially, scientific man relies on experimentation. The time of Galileo and Newton represents a significant watershed in the process of obtaining scientific knowledge. Before their time the major emphasis was placed on revealed truth—just speculate on nature and lo and behold the inner order or "workings" of it would appear. After them, however, the emphasis was placed on experimental truth, learning about the natural world by testing, probing, experimenting, and manipulating it in a controlled manner. Certainly this is a simplified way of looking at it, but it does help us to see that such a framework of thought leads man directly to the possibility of creating an environment rather than just responding to the one inherited from Mother Nature. Of course, the ability to create an environment also carries with it the corresponding ability to destroy it. Unfortunately there is the chance that in his exhilaration at what he can do, man will end up destroying rather than creating. This is a truth we are only now vaguely realizing as important in our rediscovery of the concept of the ecosystem or the invention of the concept of Spaceship Earth.

In addition to a method of questioning and experimenting, the search for order is a distinguishing mark of the scientific endeavor. Perhaps at its very core it would be correct to describe science as an activity that puts order into experience. There is no single way or magical method that must be followed to do this. I do not happen to subscribe to the belief that there is an all-powerful scientific method that because of its inherent objectivity imparts to its users a special and high place in the search for truth. The order that one sees in the context of a given body of information, whether it be a set of data in numbers or the observation of the interplay betweeen people, is quite a personal thing that is perceived in the mind of the perceiver. This is not to say that there is no such thing as order upon which we can agree; rather, I am saying that we should recognize that two persons may perceive different things in the same experience. Or to say it more colloquially, some see the same glass as half full and others as half empty. Creativity is not a phenomenon peculiar to any single segment of man's knowledge. It cannot be pinned down to one set of principles. In other words the creative person is one who can see an order or relationship that is not there or he can look at one thing and see another. Without this kind of creativity, science, as well as literature, religion, etc., would have all closed up shop long ago and we would now be sunning ourselves on the beach, content in the fullness of knowledge.

Perhaps the distinguishing mark of science, in regard to order, is that it does strive toward universal agreement in an attempt to build a foundation of agreed upon knowledge as a basis for continual search. There are many examples in science where the paradigm or model that has become widely accepted is successfully challenged and replaced by another view or model. In a nutshell, this is the real excitement of science—creating new order. But this is really nothing different from the other spheres of man's intellectual, emotional, or artistic searches.

Nevertheless, in the activity of creating order there is one criterion that is inviolable: science shall be truthful. However, truth is not the blank record of facts; it is the search for order within those facts. Scientific truth does not refer to the truth or falsity of individual facts or pieces of information but rather it refers to the truth of the laws or relationships one sees within those facts, i.e., the order. And there are two crucial points: truth may change as one's experience changes and truth is *not* self-evident, it rests on an act of human judgment. It is by an act of choice that one decides what law or relationship he sees within the facts before him. He then acts on that truth and uses it until some new experience compels him to change it. So contrary to popular opinion, science is not a purely objective endeavor. Scientists strive to be as objective as possible in their observations; however, human values necessarily enter into the choice of truth since no one can choose outside of his particular set of values or previous framework of knowledge. Indeed, the great success of science is really bound up in the fact that its truth does change. Everything in science is open to question; everything is subject to scrutiny and testing. It is not a mark of shame for truth to change in science, it is the peak of creativity to change it. Change is the hallmark of the whole endeavor. And who can argue that such a process has not been incredibly successful at understanding Mother Nature? Now the process proposes to conquer Mother Nature.

The sum of all this is to say that science is really a framework for viewing the physical world. Man cannot be separated from his science. Science is not only something that one does in a laboratory. In a broader sense, science is a way of living, a way of meeting and responding to the world. It is something that pervades all of one's life and thinking because its basic roots lie in experience and in the way in which he relates to the world around him.

THE NEW RULES
OF THE GAME

There are two additional things about science that it seems to me have not been very widely understood. First, the general direction of science has changed from that of "finding" to "doing" and second, the actual rules for the game of life are currently being discovered. This carries with it the corollary ability of being able to do things in a totally new way. The first point will be discussed here; to convince you on the second is the aim of the chapters that follow.

No doubt it is evident to all of us that the major agent in the phenomenon of accelerated change has been science, but I am not sure that we fully understand a subtle but quite profound change in the direction of science that has taken root in the past one hundred years or so. The great scientists of the past three hundred years, for example, Newton, Dalton, and Darwin, were all consumed by a desire to discover the secrets of nature. Their main interest was in collecting data and information about the natural world with the goal of organizing it into knowledge frameworks that told us the way things operate (Newton's laws of motion), the way things are made (Dalton's atomic theory), or the way things came to be (Darwin's explanation of the origin of the many species). To be sure, science is still greatly interested in basic information about the natural world, but somewhere in the past one hundred years or so a new major driving force developed in science which asks: What can we *do* with this knowledge of the natural world? What can we *do* with nature? And as soon as we use the verb "do," we are in a choice and value situation. I do not mean to say that applied science has appeared only recently. Rather, the point is that a major thrust in modern-day science is to ask questions about what we can do with our knowledge today, not only so that we will be in a position to *know* something new tomorrow, but also so that we will be able to change the world and the way in which we *do* things tomorrow. In a word, modern science has become future-oriented, and in a phrase, the value implications of the use of science, whether we like it or not, are now an integral part of the scientific endeavor.

The *value* questions must be asked in the same framework as the *how* questions. This is not to say that they are the same kind of question, but to deal with one and not the other is no longer possible. For the most part, I believe, our present ecological and technological crises (such as popollution and the spiraling arms race) can be attributed to this failure to recognize this new framework. This means that we must face up to the ethical and value concerns and infuse them into the framework of science, not to control what is studied or how, but rather to bring into the mainstream of decision-making the question of how the knowledge is to be used.

Please do not read this to mean that I am suggesting that we can solve our problems without more science or that we should reduce our scientific efforts. This would be a disastrous move (unless we are willing to return to the Stone Age). I am arguing for an ecological awareness of the fact that we live in an equilibrium situation in which wiping out or changing one factor in that balance inevitably has impact at other points. Yes, we need more information, not less, to solve our problems. But we must learn how to avoid falling into the trap of easy thinking of "instant" solutions such as replacing the "bad" phosphates in detergents with the "good" NTA. The complexity and scale of dealing with an ecosystem as a whole unit (whether it be a forest or a city) forces us to realize that adding *anything* by the tons to our water supply is going to have *some* effect. To look for a safe and harmless additive is a pipe dream. Every move of man, as well as nature, has an impact on the whole of nature. So before we try to create a new biological or psychological man, we had better do some serious contemplation.

INTERFACE BETWEEN SCIENCE
AND SOCIETY

But what does all this have to do with society? Since World War II we have seen an incredible increase in the use of scientific knowledge for what has loosely been termed "in the service of man" or "better living through chemistry." The examples are familiar: fertilizers for food, drugs for disease, pesticides for pests, and weapons for war. But we have demanded and used this science without seriously asking the question of how this knowledge impinges on our lives as individuals and as groups, i.e., as a society. So, in a nutshell, the science and society interface is one that calls us to face up to the implications of what has been called the technological imperative —the notion that if you can do it, do it. But as we have noted the theologian and ethicist Paul Ramsey reminds us, "There may be a number of things that we *can* do that *ought* not to be done." [8] This does not imply an anti-intellectual position or a pessimistic suppression of knowledge and science. I am arguing that our educational ethos, as well as that of society, must begin to develop ways of paying attention to the implications and value spin-offs from the use of science *before, during,* and *after* we do something. It is no argument, however, that we should not do something because we don't know what will happen.

If we grant that the pivotal point is responsibility, the next question is, Whose responsibility? Barry Commoner, a leading eco-spokesman, stated: "No scientific principle, though, can tell us what we should value more, the shade of the elm tree or the song of the robin. Public policy—to spray or not to spray—is a value judgment, not a scientific question." [9] This is a laudable sentiment, but it is not realistic to expect that it will be possible for scientists to hand specialized and complex information over to ordinary citizens and then sit back and let them make the decisions. Therefore the creative challenge of the future in this regard is to blend together the concerns of the public and the knowledge of science. This is not to say that one does not have the other (i.e., public does not have knowledge and science does not have concern), but it is to say we must develop new modes of decision-making. And to make a long story short, and to anticipate the argument in the concluding chapter, we cannot truly begin to build this new framework of decision-making and responsibility until we develop a new kind of man. Man as he is today or was yesterday provides abundant proof that he cannot handle the greed-drive inherent in the heritage of the "self-made" man or the pioneer spirit of individualization. The isolated and individual man is an impossibility in the web of modern society.

As long as we continue to act in either ignorance or deliberate inattention to others, we are not going to be able to solve the problems of the use of modern science. As Garret Hardin has argued, we live in a "commons" in which the actions of each individual does affect the group.[10] If one hundred farmers share the same field and each farmer has one hundred cattle grazing on it, it is in the interests of each individual to add an additional steer to the common grazing ground. But if each individual does this, then the one hundred additional cattle double the grazing power and eventually the "commons" is destroyed by overgrazing; thus, all the individuals go down. The same argument applies for the population problem. We are in a new age, and the only way out, in my view, is to generate a new blend of cooperation. I like the way Teilhard de Chardin puts it: "No evolutionary future awaits man except in association with all other men." [11] Until the realization comes that what I do has an impact on you, we will not be able to begin to deal with the future in which the rules of the game will be changed.

"GO HE MUST"

I am not predicting a doomsday. I am, however, trying to predict some serious problems unless we face up to the awesome responsibilities on our doorstep. To conclude this attempt to provide a perspective on scientific man, I would like to turn to one of the most imaginative writers of science fiction, H. G. Wells. Although the story *The First Men in the Moon* dates back to 1901, it contains a message about modern science and the spirit of man which is quite illuminating for our day and for the future since it points up both man's dilemma and his inextinguishable faith.

The story is about Mr. Cavor, a scientist, and his cohort, Mr. Bedford, a businessman who had stumbled upon Cavor merely by chance. Cavor devises a method of transportation based on gravity resistance which they use to carry them to the moon. In their excitement of leaping about in the moon's weak gravity field (shades of our Apollo astronauts) they become lost from their spaceship and soon are captured by the Selenite inhabitants of the moon. As they contemplate their fate, chained in a room beneath the surface, Bedford vents his frustration by lashing out at science and pointing to the dilemma of the change it produces.

> It's this accursed Science. . . . It's the very Devil. The medieval priests and persecutors were right, and the moderns are all wrong. You tamper with it and it offers you gifts. And directly you take them it knocks you to pieces in some unexpected way. Old passions and new weapons—now it upsets your religion, now it upsets your social ideas, now it whirls you off to desolation and misery.[12]

After a violent escape from their confinement the two men decide to separate in their search for the space capsule. Alone with his thoughts and in a more mellow mood, Bedford asks the question, Why had they come to the moon?

> The thing presented itself to me as a perplexing problem. What is this spirit in man that urges him for ever to depart from happiness and security, to toil, to place himself in danger, even to risk a reasonable certainty of death? It dawned upon me up there in the moon as a thing I ought always to have known, that man is not made simply to go about being safe and comfortable and well fed and amused. Against his interest, against his happiness he is constantly being driven to do unreasonable things. Some force not himself impels him and go he must.[13]

Is that not the true measure of man—"go he must"? The direction of science for the past four hundred years has been a deep and inner response to a query about just what kind of physical world we live in. And the success of this endeavor is without parallel in the annals of intellectual history. Man's exploration has ranged from the quark and the inner regions of the atom to the moon and the outer regions of intergalactic space. But the real importance and import of this quest has not been the catalogs of fact and information that have resulted. Rather, it has been the spirit of an endeavor that has pervaded man's intellect and is threatening to pick him up by his own bootstraps and place him on a new evolutionary level. What we have seen labeled as scientific change has been great indeed. But consider what man is about to do now. He is looking into the very depths of his soul and is beginning to ask what it is that makes him man.

What are we to say about the "force" or "spirit" that impels man to go on? Is it due to nothing more than the inevitable outcome of man's gathering of new knowledge, or is it due to the mysterious God force, the omnipotent Creator? What is it that drives man inexhaustibly to seek new knowledge, even in the face of death? The answer will not be found in the knowledge of science, but it is a question that man as a creature cannot ignore.

Nonetheless, in the early morning light the spirit of man invariably rises with the sun and proclaims—go he must! The Future is waiting to be born: shall we go?

2

Mood Drugs

Chemical mood changers are a part of our confrontation with life. It is a rare person who does not use some type of chemical substance—whether it be a yearly dose of Grandma's spring tonic, a monthly trip on LSD, a weekend binge on alcohol, an occasional aspirin, or daily drinks of caffeine—in an attempt to improve the quality of his mood, and thus of life itself. To be sure, man's attempts at mood-changing have always been an integral part of his past, perhaps from the moment he first discovered that he had a mouth. Yet in our day we are confronted with a radically new dimension of drug use. Instead of chewing coca leaves or boiling tonics out of roots, each of which contains a multitude of different chemicals, we now encapsulate in pills single pure substances that we isolate from nature or synthesize in the laboratory. By the simple and quick act of swallowing a pill, we can achieve a specific kind of desirable action or chemical nirvana. The exact number is not known, but one ball-park estimate is that one third of the adult American population has a prescription for some kind of "mood-altering" drug.

In searching for the significance of the cultural change from "chewing leaves" to "popping pills," it seems to me that any way we turn confronts us with numerous difficulties. A college student once wrote to me: "If life is as I think, a search for oneself, then one should never stop searching. But then again, if I use drugs, this removes me from other people." Compare this to a prediction made recently by a group of British scientists that by 1990 there will be "synthetic mood modifiers, pacifiers, and general 'comforters'" which "may challenge the traditional role of tobacco and alcohol and offer less hazardous alternatives to drugs such as marihuana and LSD." In other words, there is the probability that "by 1990 the social use of medicines will have become accepted as legitimate," just as "tea, coffee, alcohol and tobacco are natural drugs whose use now is socially acceptable." [1] We are confronted with a situation in which certain types of drug use alienate one person from another, yet we know that drugs not only are widely used in our society but in the future they will be even more widely available. Does this mean increased alienation between different segments of society and isolation into two camps, or does it signify a new kind of social drug scene in which different drugs will be served as hors d'oeuvres at social gatherings?

Or look at it from another point of view—the numbers game. In 1970 more than 225 million prescriptions for mind-affecting drugs were filled by pharmacists in this country (up from 166 million in 1965). Contrast this with the fact that a recent California survey of 86 households turned up a total of 2,539 drugs (an average of 30 per household), of which only one fifth were prescription items, the other four fifths being of the self-prescribed, over-the-counter variety. Does this mean it is more acceptable to self-prescribe anything you can buy rather than to turn to medical advice? Dr. Stanley Yolles, the director of the National Institute of Mental Health, has estimated that some 8 to 12 million Americans have used marijuana on some basis, with perhaps 80 to 120 thousand of them being regular users. No matter what our views might be on marijuana, we cannot help being impressed with the magnitude of those numbers. What does it mean that large numbers of people are also unwilling to accept legal advice in restriction of drug use?

But wait a minute, someone shouts. The purpose of medical and legal guidelines is to draw the line so people will not harm themselves. This is certainly true, but is it not also true that the lines we do draw are based as much on custom as on medical knowledge, and that in reality they are a rather wiggly form of medical gerrymandering? Alcohol and tobacco, both clearly implicated in serious health problems, are on one side, the acceptable, whereas chewing coca leaves and drinking bhang (a form of marijuana), also with their health problems, are on the other. Research: that's the answer. Certainly. But have you ever wondered how we came to understand the health problems related to alcohol and tobacco use? This has come not from a few lab tests, but from years of meticulous data-gathering on people using them continually in many different quantities. And even in the face of this vast amount of information, the strongest response we have been able to generate is to remove cigarette advertising from the TV.

We need to look without prejudice at some of the

knowledge we have about five different classes of mood drugs. For the dilemma we face is not so much the contemporary hue and cry over the ancient marijuana, as it is the fact that modern pharmaceutical and medical research is turning out capsules of new chemicals at a rather fast clip, with no end in sight. It is not so much that the drug genie is now out of the bottle; he has been out for centuries. It is that now we are making our drugs on the basis of careful molecular planning and specifications. So until we can clear the fog of previous judgment about the relative evils or goods of the plethora of drugs already available, we will not be in a position to develop an ethic for responsibly accepting the reality of the sometimes subtle and sometimes profound mood changes that are, and will be, increasingly available from the simple act of "popping a pill."

Before talking about specific drug classes, please bear with the teacher in me long enough to define a few terms. The reason for this is my belief that a good deal of our difficulty in seeing the drug scene clearly and nonjudgmentally arises from the hangover of what I call the "addict" image. Addict is not a neutral word; it implies images of sin, filth, crime, immorality, and the classic pusher who stands, with collar up around his ears, waiting to prey on unsuspecting young children as they leave the school playground while he whispers, "Hey, kid, wanna try something great?" Certainly there are criminal elements in the drug scene with profit as their only motive, but the chances are much greater today that your pusher will be your friend and not a stranger. Therefore, in this discussion we shall avoid this loaded word and talk instead in terms of drug dependence and drug abuse.

By drug dependence we mean a particular state or condition that arises in a person if he self-administers a drug on a periodic or continual basis. Although there are two aspects to the phenomenon of drug dependence— physical and psychological—it is important to realize that the characteristics of a specific case depend upon the particular drug in question. Thus, we talk about alcohol dependence, marijuana dependence, etc., each implying a different set of controlling parameters. Physical dependence, or physiological dependence, means that if the administration of the drug is stopped for any reason, a general but characteristic pattern of physiological disturbances will result—ranging, say, from mild feelings of discomfort and nausea to strong responses of cramps, convulsions, and delusions. The presence of withdrawal symptoms, that is the physical reaction resulting from stopping use of the drug, is an inevitable part of physical dependence.

Psychological or psychic dependence means that the driving force for taking the drug is that it provides a feeling of satisfaction and well-being. When the drug is not available and it is wanted, suffering results from mental discomfort and anxiety (but without a pattern of physiological withdrawal symptoms). In general, any drug that produces physical dependence also seems to carry along with it the psychological effect. The reverse is not true, as I can illustrate by my psychological dependence on Pepsi-Cola, which is to say that I might miss my daily Pepsi (or two or three) but I don't suffer any detrimental physical effects as a result.

Drug habituation has also become a fairly common term, particularly since it describes the characteristics of much of the use of caffeine products and for some use of tobacco. In the setting of repeated consumption of the drug, it can be appropriately labeled as habituation if the following four conditions are met: (1) a desire, but not compulsion, to take the drug; (2) no tendency to increase the dose as time goes by; (3) some degree of psychological, but not physical, dependence; and (4) if detrimental effects are present, they are primarily on the individual using the drug.

The last set of terms are drug use and drug abuse. Perhaps it will be best to say what the latter means and then say that drug use is anything else! When we use the words "drug abuse" we are implying a situation in which the user of the drug uses it in an excessive or often compulsive manner *so that* the situation becomes detrimental to the individual's health or social or vocational adjustment. If my use of Pepsi-Cola should get to the point where I could not function in my job or where I neglected proper eating habits or ignored my family, then it would be proper to talk in terms of drug abuse. The important thing to note is that drug abuse carries with it the connotation of some detriment to the individual. A few years ago there was a case where a major-league baseball pitcher was told to stop drinking cola drinks or he would lose his job. Perhaps this could be considered as the "mildest" level of drug abuse. Also it should go without saying that the detrimental use of something like heroin can have far greater consequences than just losing a job. In short, there are degrees of drug abuse, which means that to be informed one must refer to the particular drug abused and the pattern of its use before one can postulate some type of action, if any is needed. Some people, for example, abuse tobacco, but they are just not about to give it up as they rationalize: "If I gotta go, then I might as well go this way as another."

Let us now turn our attention to five classes of mood drugs: (1) stimulants, (2) tranquilizers, (3) depressants, (4) narcotics, (5) hallucinogens, with the objective of trying to understand the amazing range of activity that is possible. For each category we shall discuss three points: accepted medical usage, mood alteration, and problems with abuse.

STIMULANTS
(also known as pep pills, pickups, and psychic energizers)

Examples: caffeine (coffee, tea, and cola drinks), nicotine (tobacco), amphetamines (Benzedrine, methamphetamine = speed), and miscellaneous (Deaner, Ritalin, Preludin, Marplan, Parnate).

Medical Usage

Because of the almost universal acceptance in our society of the individual's right to a personal decision on the use or nonuse of caffeine and tobacco products, neither of these substances has generally been thought of as a drug. Since they are so freely available and advertised, they are not generally considered a part of the modern drug lexicon. Any reference from the medical point of view is likely to take the form of a suggestion to stop using them with the reasons ranging from skipping the last cup of coffee before bedtime in order to help get a good night's sleep to the more serious suggestion that stopping smoking will relieve a current set of acute symptoms and thus lengthen one's expected life-span.

Whereas caffeine and tobacco are basically self-prescribed drugs, amphetamines and other miscellaneous stimulants are available legitimately only by doctor's prescription. Amphetamines are used in a variety of situations: to reduce fatigue, to relieve minor mental depression, to aid in dieting (perhaps more by providing a better mood and willpower to stop eating than by appetite depression), to counteract narcolepsy (an uncontrollable desire to sleep), and to help hyperkinetic children overcome the debilitating effects of their overactivity. The miscellaneous stimulants are generally used in serious situations involving long-term effects of mental states such as severe depression and apathy toward responding to one's environment.

A great deal of discussion is currently being focused in the medical community on the effectiveness of amphetamines when used as diet aids. The number of doctors who doubt its efficacy in this regard seems to be growing rapidly. Considerable attention has also been focused on the use of certain stimulants to help hyperkinetic children calm down to the point where they can cope with their overactivity (e.g., Tofranil, Ritalin, and amphetamines). The paradoxical ability of a stimulant to have a "calming" effect is still without good explanation. Perhaps it is due to the stimulant being able to help the child cope with or not be adversely affected by what is to him an overwhelming bombardment of signals from his environment. That is to say, by blocking out messages about fatigue, discomfort, and/or hunger which seem to interfere with normal activity, the child can better adapt to his environment. The controversy has centered around the right of school officials and teachers to recommend giving overactive children this kind of medication so they will be less of a problem in school and better able to respond to learning.

Mood Alteration

Obviously the stimulants are desired for their ability to perk up or enhance one's mood and outlook on life. However, there can be a variety of individual motivations involved which run the gamut from the widely accepted custom of the mid-morning coffee break (which often includes a cigarette), to the continual ingestion of large numbers of amphetamines to keep awake or to escape another dull day, or to attempting to push one's mental consciousness to new heights of stimulated sensation. Chain smoking or drinking coffee generally does not cause overstimulation; however, increased doses of amphetamines can lead to wild exaggeration of normal effects in terms of excitability, talkativeness, tremors, and extreme variations in mental states.

In the mid-1960's Preludin (used orally for appetite depression) became quite a problem in Sweden on the basis of two effects which could be produced by injection: massive heightening of all sensations and an aphrodisiac action (sexual stimulation). The mood alteration of the first type is no doubt genuine; however, the second action appears to be mythical or at least more attributable to "suggestion" rather than drug activity.

Problems with Abuse

The situations with regard to caffeine and tobacco are well known. Both may be in the category of psychological dependence for a given individual, but it is also clear that long-term use of tobacco (especially inhaling cigarette smoke) is intimately associated with serious health problems of cardiovascular disease, bronchitis, and lung cancer. Regular therapeutic use of amphetamines is not a procedure that leads to health difficulties (as long as one sticks to the recommended dosages). However, the other extreme of "popping" thirty to forty pills a day or mainlining a few cc's every three or four hours, both in order to produce "runs" or "speeding" for up to four or five days of continual mental and physical excitation, is clearly recognized as having the ability to result eventually in a severely deteriorated health situation. An additional factor is that a lethergic feeling after awakening from a "run" often serves as a stimulus to start another.

The miscellaneous category of stimulants includes potent and sometimes unpredictable drugs. They should be used only under conditions of constant medical supervision as there is the possibility of toxic effects to the liver, brain, and cardiovascular system, and of numerous complications such as convulsions, tremors, insomnia, and high blood pressure. For example, death has been known to occur from the combination of some of these drugs with the eating of cheese.

In the case of Preludin, mentioned earlier, there are serious complications of severe psychoses with excessive intravenous use. This is the same problem that exists with injection abuse of amphetamines and is perhaps the source of the hippie saying: "Speed Kills."

TRANQUILIZERS

Examples: antipsychotic: Rauwolfia alkaloids (Serpasil = reserpine), Phenothiazines (Thorazine = chlorpromazine, Compazine); antineurotic: Miltown (Equanil), Librium, Valium, Frenquel, various barbiturates.

Medical Usage

The number of persons receiving some type of mental treatment has been increasing slowly but steadily over the past few decades. However, since about 1955 there has been coupled with this growth the curious phenomenon of a decrease in the numbers of persons resident in mental hospitals. The explanation can be summarized in one word—tranquilizers. Up until the 1950's the only thing that could be done with an overagitated person was physically to restrain him via a straitjacket or padded room or to use chemical restraint via a sedative or hypnotic drug that would put him to sleep. From the simplest point of view the overall effect of a tranquilizing drug is to reduce mental anxiety without at the same time reducing ability to function in a conscious manner. Thus the introduction of tranquilizers literally produced a revolution in the treatment of mentally ill persons since the straitjackets could be stored in the padded rooms while new chemicals calmed the patient (without puting him to sleep) so that psychotherapy could be inaugurated and maintained.

No one has yet devised a universally acceptable scheme for classifying the various tranquilizers. Some schemes use pharmacological action and others clinical application or even chemical structure. However, for our purposes we will use the labels antipsychotic and antineurotic (understanding that this is not a clear differential and that some tranquilizers overlap the two categories). By psychotic we mean a mental disorder in which there is serious disorganization of the personality. In general there does not have to be a stress situation for this disorder to be evident. In contrast, a neurotic is a person who responds abnormally to a stressful situation which links in his mind a relationship to some unpleasant experience in the past. In general the neurotic's contact with reality is good; however, a stressful situation may overwhelm him with persistent fears and anxieties, frequently evidenced by unexplainable aches and pains, insomnia, and weird phobias. He is often unable to cope with ordinary problems in effective ways. (I once heard a description of the difference between the two: a psychotic is a person who thinks that $2 + 2 = 5$, and a neurotic is a person who knows that $2 + 2 = 4$, but he worries about it!)

Again with the use of general terms it would be helpful to indicate how each group works. The antipsychotic drugs have a direct action on various levels of the brain and central nervous system. One model is derived from the ability of the drug to affect the sorting mechanism in the brain which is responsible for filtering impulses before they impinge on higher centers in the brain. So in terms of a crude analogy, this type of tranquilizer works by acting as a sort of volume control reducing the flow of impulses to the brain, and thereby "calming" the individual. The antineurotic drugs can be thought of in terms of two kinds of action, one a muscle relaxant effect and the other sedation via a mild state of central nervous system depression. From the point of view of the muscle relaxant effect the idea is that when a person is anxious and agitated his muscles are "tight" and unrelaxed. When this kind of tranquilizer relaxes the muscles, or cuts down the number of signals going from the muscles to the brain, the effect on one's mental state is similar to the feeling of kicking off one's shoes and plopping down into a comfortable chair at the end of a rough day.

To sum up: the medical use of the antipsychotic drugs is in situations of severe personality disorders and schizophrenic symptoms such as delusions or hallucinations, and the antineurotic drugs are called for in the treatment of tension and anxiety arising from minor unresolved, subconscious conflicts or for nervous hyperexcitability or tension resulting from excessive stimulation by one's environment.

Mood Alteration

No doubt tension and anxiety have been a problem for man ever since he started living in groups. The only alternative the caveman had, if his frustrations reached the breaking point, was to leave the group and face the trials of nature and saber-toothed tigers alone. Modern man, however, has only to visit his doctor in the hopes of getting a ticket for one of hundreds of different pills stocked on the shelves of his neighborhood pharmacy. And the truly incredible thing is that this modern method of mood alteration can run the spectrum from tension centered around coping with a new job to severe mental agitation to the point of screaming, violent fits of fury.

In order to illustrate the types of mood alteration available with tranquilizers we can turn to the pages of drug advertisement that abound in medically oriented journals. In one case a full-page picture of an attractive, but worried-looking, young woman with an armful of books is accompanied by the following statements: "To help free her of excessive anxiety"; "Exposure to new friends and other influences may force her to reevaluate herself and her goals"; and "Her newly stimulated intellectual curiosity may make her more sensitive to and apprehensive about unstable national and world conditions." Further along in the text it suggests that this particular tranquilizer, in conjunction with counseling and reassurance, "can help the anxious student to handle the primary problem and to 'get her back on her feet.' " [2]

The same type of approach is used with younger children as the following quotations used in connection with a picture of a tearful litle girl illustrate: "School, the dark, separation, dental visits, 'monsters' "; "The everyday anxieties of childhood sometimes get out of hand"; and "A child can usually deal with his anxieties. But sometimes the anxieties overpower the child. Then, he needs your help. Your help may include . . . [tranquilizer x]." [3]

The need for mood changes has also been linked to the currently popular ecology issue as one ad is titled: "Environmental Depression." It goes on to say: "Air conditioners are turned down, or off. Lights dim. Transportation slows down, or stops—usually in a long hot summer. This is when comfort, conveniences, and productivity suffer. So does the emotional outlook of some individuals. Already frustrated by the constant din around them, helpless in the face of situations they can't control, and faced with the daily exposure to bad news and crises, they fall prey to a phenomenon of the times— one that may overwhelm the patient and may cause symptoms of mild depression to occur more frequently." [4]

Even the time-honored institution of marriage fits into the mood picture as a full-page picture of a bride's perplexed and anxious face is accompanied by the opening words: "Wish the newlywed happiness. And a new course of therapy that brings her hypertension under control." [5]

These advertisements leave no doubt that one of the major directed uses of tranquilizers today is to allay and relieve the everyday anxieties and tensions of living in our complex, modern world.

Problems with Abuse

Under ordinary conditions of therapeutic use, problems with antineurotic tranquilizers can be solved by the prescribing physician. However, long-term abuse at higher than usual doses has been linked with physical dependence characteristics. The barbiturate drugs have a serious limitation in that overdoses can result in death, but situations have been known where 50–90 therapeutic doses of Miltown were taken at one time without resultant suicidal death. On the other hand, the antipsychotic tranquilizers are potent drugs which must be used under close medical supervision. As an illustration, reserpine can activate latent peptic ulcers and in some situations can cause a depression so serious as to create a possibility of suicide.

DEPRESSANTS

Examples: ethyl alcohol and barbiturates (phenobarbital, Nembutal, Seconal).

Medical Usage

Alcohol is like caffeine and tobacco in that it is one of the widely self-prescribed drugs in our society. Although once medically important as an anesthetic, it might be fair to say today that many doctors would be more likely to recommend against its use than in its favor. Barbiturates, on the other hand, hold a prominent and important place in modern medicine as evidenced by the fact that approximately one million pounds of barbiturates are produced each year—enough to supply approximately twenty-four 100-mg doses to every man, woman, and child in the country. They are used as sleeping pills and for some types of mental problems, particularly in short-term relief of anxiety symptoms.

Mood Alteration

The cocktail party is the classic example of mood alteration in American society. Anyone who has ever been to one must surely have been struck by the wide variety of mood responses that can be elicited in an evening of social drinking—ranging from sulking and self-pity to a state of frequent, loquacious outbursts. In general terms, the heavy drinker can be thought of as a person who approaches problems by the method of "acting out" frustrations due to aggression, sexuality, or inability to accept one's own personality. In effect this person participates in a kind of outer-directed behavior which may be quite visible in terms of the party drunk who smashes up the place or quietly observed in the sullen inebriate in the corner who is feeling sorry for himself while projecting his troubles onto everyone who is too busy with their own problems to listen to him.

The mood alteration provided by barbiturates is quite similar to that caused by alcohol, and in fact, the best way to distinguish between a "barbiturate drunk" and an "alcoholic drunk" is to note the presence or absence of an alcohol smell on the breath.

Problems with Abuse

As with tobacco, the American public seems to be well educated on the effect of long-term usage of alcohol, although there is scanty evidence in either case to suggest that many are willing to act on that knowledge and do something about it. Alcohol has been clearly implicated in situations of crime (of the persons in prison, alcohol played a role in half of the criminal acts that put them there), automobile accidents (half of the deaths and injuries are attributable to alcohol consumption as one of the causal factors), numerous industrial and home accidents, and countless episodes of violence. All these situations have an impact on the individual as well as society. In personal terms, long-term usage can lead to physical and psychological dependence, brain damage, cirrhosis of the liver, and a general breakup of health.

The problems with barbiturates are similar to those of alcohol. Overdosing with barbiturates can be readily achieved (say twelve doses of phenobarbital at one time), and thus they are often used as a suicide agent. However, accidental suicide also occurs when people mix the consumption of alcohol and barbiturates, as both are central nervous system depressants. Physical dependence can result from barbiturate abuse, and abrupt withdrawal is a life-threatening situation. The withdrawal syndrome includes muscular weakness, nausea, insomnia, major motor seizures, and on the third to seventh day, psychotic reactions resembling delirium tremens of alcoholism or schizophrenic behavior.

Narcotics

Examples: opium, morphine, heroin, Demerol, codeine.

Medical Usage

The beginnings of the use of the dried milky exudate from the unripe seed pods of the poppy plant, called opium, is buried somewhere in the unkept records of prehistoric man. There are many references to the use of opium to relieve pain and provide euphoria (sense of well-being) in the historical records of the major cultures. One of the ingredients of opium, morphine, was first isolated in 1803, and it is amazing to contemplate that this antique material is still today, even in the face of modern chemical miracles, the drug of choice for the relief of pain, especially dull and unrelenting pain. No doubt this is due to a unique set of properties of the drug action of morphine: a depression of the ability to perceive pain and the presence of a euphoria or "high" which reduces the concern for the pain. Heroin, a synthetic derivative of morphine (i.e., not a naturally occurring ingredient of opium), came along in the late

1800's, and because of its ability to relieve the withdrawal symptoms of morphine, it was hailed as a cure for the dependence problems associated with that painkiller. But alas, it was soon discovered that heroin had physical dependence properties of its own, and because it is not superior to morphine as a pain reliever, medical science put it back on the shelf. Demerol is a synthetic pain-killer that is not as potent as morphine and which produces less euphoria. It is sometimes used as a substitute for morphine, but it is also a drug that produces physical dependence. Codeine is another alkaloid derived from the poppy plant, but because its analgesic action is only one tenth that of morphine it is used only for minor pain or perhaps more commonly as an antitussive (anticough) medication.

Mood Alteration

Some of the characteristic adjectives used to describe the mood of narcotic abusers are nonaggressive, passive, withdrawn, and lethargic. Thus one would naturally ask about what kinds of forces, characteristics of personality, or views of the world would produce the motivation to seek this kind of mood-state, particularly in the light of the fact that it involves a seemingly endless treadmill of continual drug use. Although there are a wide variety of problems that confront any individual in the ghetto and lower socioeconomic groups (where the vast majority of abusers are found), it does seem reasonable to understand their motivation toward narcotics in terms of an attempt to see a solution to their conflicts by withdrawing into a passive and lethargic existence where reality is largely blotted out. In other words, the solution involves a withdrawal from society and its demands for living. There is also an element (sometimes conscious, sometimes not) of attacking society for creating the problem, in that the narcotic abuser must turn to crime and illegal activities in order to find the funds to support a use level that can require from ten to one hundred dollars a day.

Toward the end of the 1960's heroin use began to show up in middle- and upper-class suburbs and penthouses. The sociological significance of the needs being fulfilled in these cases is not yet certain. One can guess, though, that life for some in the goods-rich suburbs is in some way as meaningless for them as it is for the typical heroin abuser in the goods-poor ghetto.

The initial mood alteration from morphine or heroin is a "high"—a "rush" sometimes described as similar to an orgasm. But after physical dependence sets in, this high often disappears, and the drug is sought only to stave off the withdrawal symptoms resulting from not taking it. Because heroin is three to four times as potent as morphine, it has become the drug of choice for narcotics abusers.

Problems with Abuse

There has never been any debate on the fact that narcotic abuse is a situation in which the individual, as well as society, must pay some kind of price, often a high one. The individual pays it through personal neglect, disruption of interpersonal relationships, the mental anguish of a constant preoccupation with the prospects for the next fix, the possible contraction of hepatitis through nonsterile injection techniques, and most seriously with the ever-present danger of an OD, an *over-dose* that can cause rapid death. This latter situation is literally a gamble taken with every injection because the street heroin is "cut" or diluted with inert substances before sale so that the percentage of heroin generally runs from 0 to 10 percent. If the mixture is rich in heroin, it is possible that the dose will be higher than the user can tolerate, the result being death through respiratory paralysis.

Society, on the other hand, pays similar and enormous costs in humane terms relating to the loss of personal relationships and withdrawal from participation in the "positive" aspects of living, as well as the practical costs in terms of crime. As a kind of ball-park estimate let us take 200,000 heroin users who need twenty-five dollars a day to purchase the needed drug. This means a *daily* change in hands of five million dollars. If all this money was raised by selling stolen goods (assuming one third of the value of the item can be recovered), then we are talking about fifteen million dollars a day of crime. By way of contrast, however, the cigarette industry pays about fifteen million dollars a day in federal taxes. The purpose of this contrast is not to pit the relative benefits or detriments of heroin against tobacco, but rather to point out that there is a great deal of hand-wringing and federal effort in the former case, and not in the latter.

The combination of physical and psychological dependence found with the abuse of narcotics has proved to be an extremely difficult one to overcome. The odds are far greater that an abuser who "kicks the habit" will eventually return to the drug as opposed to staying "clean." A currently popular method of drug therapy is to substitute a single daily oral dose of methadone for the multiple injections of heroin. This does seem to allow the narcotics abuser to stabilize his emotional and physical life to the point of being able to develop new, positive habits. The unfortunate part is that the person becomes dependent on the methadone; however, it is felt that eventual release from its dependence can be accomplished without difficulty after the person has developed a new life-style.

HALLUCINOGENS

Examples: LSD, peyote (mescaline), psilocybin, dimethyltryptamine (DMT), STP (Serenity, Tranquility, and Peace), marijuana (pot), and THC (tetrahydrocannabinol—active ingredient of marijuana).

Medical Usage

At this stage of the game none of the hallucinogens is a part of the prescription bag of your local doctor. However, a great deal of study has been done with clinical possibilities of LSD, and there is the likelihood that one day LSD, or a similar drug, will be available by prescription and medical supervision. The major investigative thrusts for the use of LSD have been in three situations: treatment of alcoholism, as an adjunct in psychotherapy, and for the relief of pain resulting from terminal cancer. Presently there appear to be three schools of thought on LSD therapy: (1) psycholytic, (2) psychedelic, and (3) psychedelic peak.

In psycholytic therapy, multiple sessions with small doses of LSD are used (25–50 micrograms). Psychotherapy is carried out with the patient before, during, and after the drug use with the aim of uncovering unconscious material which can subsequently be analyzed (either under the influence of the drug or not). The therapy labeled psychedelic involves limited psychotherapy, either in preparation or follow-up, but not during the time of drug action. The idea here is to have a single session with a relatively high dose (200 micrograms or more) in the hopes that the user will have a "big" experience which will allow him to reorganize spontaneously his value system and outlook on life. The third method, psychedelic peak, involves components of both of the preceding methods in that there is intensive psychotherapy prior to use of the LSD in relatively high dose. The goal is to provide a setting and direction for the experience so that a peak or transcendental experience results (defined further later on). There is generally no therapy during the "trip," but if the peak experience provides meaningful emotional insight into the basic self-worth of the patient (a kind of self-understanding), then this is capitalized on in subsequent psychotherapy.

Marijuana is under intensive investigation at this time. However, the major emphasis or thrust seems to be directed toward discovering whether or not there are ill effects of short- or long-term usage rather than toward uncovering possible medical usages. It is interesting to note that in 1840, O'Shaughnessy, a British physician, wrote about the use of marijuana as an analgesic, anticonvulsant, and muscle relaxant. Indeed, it has been widely used in medical practice; however, its popularity reached a peak about the time of World War I, after which its use declined considerably. Even so, in 1916 the eighth edition of a medical textbook referred to Cannabis (the Latin name for the marijuana or hemp plant is *Cannabis sativa*) as a most satisfactory remedy for migraine headache.

Mood Alteration

In a word, LSD is incredible as a mood alterer. On the basis of the extremely small doses used, it is no doubt the most potent drug known to mankind. Dosage levels are on the microgram scale, and to get an idea of the tiny nature of this amount, the next time you take an aspirin tablet pause long enough to look at it: if it was pure LSD, there would be enough chemical there for over three thousand separate effective doses. If you have the evening free, try dividing the tablet into that many parts!

The mechanism of LSD action is unknown; however, in nontechnical descriptive terms various people have described it as having an effect on the filtering mechanism that allows sensory input into the brain (obviously greatly enhancing the flow of impressions), removing a translucent screen before one's eyes, or resulting in "incredibly intensified perceptions." No doubt it is quite difficult to appreciate the impact of this mind expansion without having the experience itself. To try to "tell it like it is," users have employed phrases such as the following: "It puts you in a different dimension. There is no way to communicate it. It dissolves the boundaries between concepts." [6] "It was like a shower on the inside." [7] "Existence was holding its breath—endlessly. . . . It wasn't that I saw the chair differently. I was the chair." [8]

Walter N. Pahnke has developed a five-element description of the major kinds of psychedelic drug experiences. It does not provide a description of the kinds of experiences to be expected from a "trip" but rather is a means of clarifying and categorizing the psychological phenomena.

Psychotic: "characterized by the intense, negative experience of fear to the point of panic, paranoid delusions of suspicion or grandeur, toxic confusion, impairment of abstract reasoning, remorse, depression, and isolation or somatic discomfort or both."

Cognitive: "characterized by astonishingly lucid thought. Problems can be seen from a novel perspective, and the inner relationships of many levels or dimensions can be seen all at once."

Aesthetic: "characterized by a change and intensification of all sensory modalities. Fascinating changes in sensations and perception can occur: synesthesia in which sounds can be 'seen,' apparent pulsations or life-like movements in objects such as flowers or stones, the appearance of great beauty in ordinary things, release of powerful emotions through music, and eyes-closed visions of beautiful scenes, intricate geometric patterns, architectural forms, historical events, and almost anything imaginable."

Psychodynamic: "characterized by a dramatic emergence into consciousness of material that was previously unconscious or preconscious."

Psychedelic peak, cosmic, transcendental, or mystical: "can be summarized under the following six major psychological characteristics: (1) sense of unity or oneness . . . , (2) transcendence of time and space, (3) deeply felt positive mood (joy, peace, and love), (4) sense of awe-someness, reverence, and wonder, (5) meaningfulness of psychological or philosophical insight or both; and (6) ineffability (sense of difficulty in communicating the experience by verbal description)." [9]

The mood alteration provided by smoking or eating marijuana is not as intense and depth-shaking as that of LSD. In a popular sense the widespread use of marijuana seems to stem from a desire to get high and to participate in a pleasurable diversion from the ordinary routine by an altering of the senses. In general, there seem to be three basic positions in regard to the "reality" exper-ienced as a result of the marijuana-induced mood alter-ation. In the first position it is held that because the drug distorts perceptions, vision, and images, any notion of reality when high is to be considered deceptive, false, unreal, and invalid. Thus the only reason for using mari-juana is for kicks and a hedonistic high. A second posi-tion, however, centers around the belief that when an individual is high, his vision of reality is "more real" than the everyday one forced on him by society (the straight situation). Therefore the use of marijuana is linked with attempts to get rid of hang-ups and to see what life is "really" all about. The third view is a com-posite one in which high and straight are held to be two different windows to reality—two alternate ways of viewing the world. Each one is legitimate, real, valid, and true on its own level, and in order truly to understand reality, one must experience both of these complemen-tary views.

We will not take space to differentiate between the other hallucinogens of DMT, STP, peyote, psilocybin, etc., and will just say in passing that they are generally like LSD but are much less potent drugs which often produce less intense experiences. Each one, however, does have its own peculiar plus and minus points.

Problems with Abuse

LSD is well known for its capacity to precipitate problems ranging from mild personality disorders to serious personality changes which can result in withdrawal from society in psychotic episodes. Flashbacks of psychedelic experiences can occur weeks or months after the last use of the drug. Human chromosomal damage has not been clearly established. Good studies over long periods of time are needed to clarify the type of risk that might be involved. On the basis of animal studies, there is some indication that LSD, taken early in pregnancy, might have adverse effects on embryonic development. Additional study is needed.

The marijuana picture is quite clouded at the moment due to the dust created by the arguments over its not being as bad as alcohol or being a surefire cause of eventual heroin abuse. It is known that a certain percentage of users will become potheads in that the use of marijuana becomes the central focus of their life. Personality disorders of all types can be a part of the picture surrounding marijuana use, including serious psychotic reactions. One point often neglected is that large numbers of people seem to be using this drug without serious short-term effects. There are many variables in the long-term picture, but this will take a few decades to sort out properly.

It is difficult to get accurate statistics on drug use;

however, in a speech late in 1970, Dr. Donald Louria, noted author and researcher on drugs, made the following estimations on the pattern of involvement with marijuana: Fifty percent of those who use it will do so for a period of weeks or months and then stop, 25 percent will continue to use it with no overt problems, 20 percent will experiment with other drugs, 4 percent will become potheads—continual users with serious psychological problems in some cases, and 1 percent will experience panic or mental problems.

SUMMARY

In closing, I want to make two points that generally have a tendency to get lost in the shuffle of drug information. First, there is no such thing as a safe or harmless drug. The action of any drug is dependent upon a complex combination of many factors, such as, dose, method of administration, age, weight, state of health, presence or absence of food or drugs in the stomach, etc. A serious problem, not only for the illicit drug scene but even for hospitals, is that of interaction from taking more than one drug at a time. Unforeseen and sometimes dangerous complications can result. For this reason medical treatment of bad trips can be difficult to prescribe. Second, the hardest string to pull out of the drug picture is the impact and importance of the expectations of the user as opposed to actual pharmacological effect. What the user expects (or fears) can often influence the mood effects.

Now, how can we sum up this survey of mood drugs? To me, the central point that comes through is the realization that there is a drug available for almost any mood-alteration situation one can think up. To state categorically that man should not use mood drugs in his confrontation with life is tantamount to sticking one's head in the sand with the ostriches. Drugs are here to stay. The question of the next chapter is, *How* should we use them? not, *Should* we use them?

3

Which Pill Shall I Take Today—
The Red or the Green?

Next time you are in a drugstore, take a few minutes to look around and try to estimate the number of different drugs and preparations that are available for purchase "over the counter," as they say. Then, if the shelves of the prescription drug section are visible behind the pharmacist's counter, try to estimate the number of different drugs available there upon presentation of the proper ticket written by a doctor (which in some cases is not hard to get). And if you like to play games, try Stump-Your-Pharmacist by trying to see if you can come up with an ailment, pain, or mood problem for which he does not have some type of pill or medicine that will "help out."

Indeed, if the panorama of drugs with highly selective as well as broad spectrum activity continues to grow at anywhere near the pace of the past twenty years, it would not be too farfetched to suggest that alongside of our vitamins, deodorant, contraceptive pills (for either sex), and hair spray (again, for either sex) there will one day soon be a set of seven decorated bottles with the following labels:

MONDAY: *Placidase* (an anti-grouch pill to tranquilize after a busy weekend and to allow for a slow reentry into the week's work)

TUESDAY: *Pepup* (a combination anti-anxiety and pep-up pill that helps to get the week rolling)

WEDNESDAY: *Inventon* (a creativity pill that lasts three days)

THURSDAY: *Endurite* (a stimulant that allows one to work for an uninterrupted stretch of ten hours)

FRIDAY: *Seducton* (a time-delayed sexual stimulant that if taken in the morning will begin to take effect at 8:00 P.M. and last for another thirty or so hours)

SATURDAY: *POPS* (a combination drug; the initials stand for *P*rogrammed *O*ccultism-*P*sychedelic *S*aturation, in other words, the latest ultimate in trips)

SUNDAY: *Divineaid* (a rapid but short acting drug whose potent spiritual effects last a little over one hour)

Even though this is suggested in a tongue in cheek manner, there might be more truth in it than we would like to allow. All of this is not said to run down the drug industry since I believe that it is responding to man's desire for medicine with which to avoid the unpleasantries of ailments of the human organism. But on the other hand, we cannot ignore the fact that this armament of drugs is changing our very way of life in ways other than providing promise of relief from stress or pain. In a nutshell the problem is this: there is almost unanimous agreement in our society that the use of drugs under a doctor's supervision is a good and beneficial thing (ignoring, of course, those small groups who feel that all medicine is foreign and unnatural). But when the issue turns to the rights of a person to "self-prescribe" these same drugs we quickly run into dozens of different shades of opinion about the freedom, or unfreedom, to use them. Unfortunately it appears that no amount of debate will ever bring us to a single acceptable point of view. As we noted earlier, drugs have been used by man ever since he first discovered he had a mouth, but it seems to me that a totally new phenomenon has arrived on a reasonably large scale within the past few decades as a spin-off of science's planned and systematic search for chemicals with specific actions in the human. The entree of the tranquilizers in the 1950's and of LSD in the 1960's has led us into a new rationale for drug use: namely, the possibility of using drugs to enhance a healthy mental state rather than to cure a sick one. I am not saying that this has never been the case before. It has, but never on the level we are now witnessing. Man has never challenged on a large scale the right of a group of licensed individuals to control what medicines all others can take. In primitive cultures the empiricism of the witch doctor ruled supreme; in our culture it is the scientific expertise of the highly educated doctor. The question is, Will this last?

What I am arguing is that we are now in the beginning stages of a new "culturization" for the use of drugs in the mainstream of life—to use drugs when one is "healthy" as well as when one is "sick." Certainly there have been many drugs used in many cultures before; however, in a general sense they can be grouped into two categories: (1) use for special religious services and rites, worship as well as war (example: peyote use by North American Indians), and (2) to tolerate harsh environmental conditions (example: coca leaf chewing by Indians in South America). But modern Western man has opened the door to a medicine chest chocked full of synthetic chemicals that can fine-tune and control mood and thus behavior. The National Institute of Health now lists over nine hundred different psychotropic drugs (i.e., tranquilizers, energizers, and hallucinogens). The cultural use of drugs is no longer limited to tribes of half-naked natives in a far-off jungle. No, the jungle is here. Drug cultures exist in all levels of our society—from the ghettos to the suburbs, from the junior highs to the colleges, from the kitchen to the office, and from the ten-year-old heroin abuser to the over-thirty swinger to the over-fifty skid row alcoholic. Prohibition was a failure as a social experiment because society did not want it. And no matter how harmful marijuana might turn out to be, if large numbers of persons continue to be willing to take the risk (as in the case of alcohol), then all the laws and special police in the land are not going to be able to deal with the situation. We are already a tobacco-alcohol culture. The question is, How many more drugs will we add? We already know the medical problems with tobacco and alcohol. Do we really think that when we know them for marijuana (and other drugs) that people will stop using them?

Surely it is not possible to boil down a complex issue like drug use into a single question. To tease the drug scene apart into its separate components is well-nigh impossible because of the cultural interrelatedness of the factors. But in my view, it comes very close to the crux of the matter if we phrase the key question in terms of discovering some kind of balance between individual freedom, on the one hand, and harm of society and the user on the other. The medicine chest is open and continually pouring forth new and shiny products, so every time we "solve" one drug problem, another drug will pop up to take its place. Therefore, we are going to have to learn how to live in a world in which they are a part of life. To deny drugs would be to deny all the health-giving powers of modern medicine, and I don't think many would be willing to do that. And saying this does not mean letting the world go to "pot." (Ugh!) Rather, it seems to me that we are compelled to take a serious look at the whole drug scene—the tobacco and the alcohol as well as the pot and the speed. If we are culturizing the use of drugs, then we should begin to try to understand our culture. Instead of focusing our attention on stopping the flow of drugs and on passing new laws, we should begin to ask ourselves: What is the state of our society and how does drug use fit into the picture?

For a long time I was convinced that education was the answer. If you could just tell people what the drugs do, then they would stop using them. But after some eight years of trying this, it has gradually dawned on me that most of those who use drugs are often quite knowledgeable about the possible effects. Indeed, they say, that's precisely why we take them—because they will cause hallucinations, cause time to slow down, increase sensory awareness by a bombardment of the senses with many inputs, etc. Education, sure, but rather than that being the "solving step" it is just the first one in a chain of understanding what another person is like, how he or she views life, and the kind of future he sees on the horizon. Only if we understand the "person" will we be able to understand the "drug." But, alas, this takes much time and effort, and "Whatthehell, in a few years they'll have to shape up and make a living," says Joe Taxpayer, while sipping beer in front of the tube watching a cigar advertisement that looks like a mirror image of the cigarette ones that are no longer allowed. How silly can we get?

I am aware that there are a lot of unstable people who get hold of drugs and get into serious trouble. But there are also many people who go into the experience with serious thought and concern. Let me illustrate the point by quoting from a paper a college student wrote concerning reasons why a drug like LSD "could be a positive factor in the lives of men if used sensibly."

> The first reason is applicable to almost any strikingly new achievement or discovery in modern society. It seems to me that the initial orientation toward any new development should be one of trying with the utmost imagination and care to think of possible valuable applications, even if those applications may involve some change in the status quo. By reacting in fear and astonishment to the possibility of significant change, men are much more likely to bring about the negative aspects they fear as well as to miss the chances for positive results. This is not to say that one should blithely forge ahead, unconscious of deleterious effects. These should be considered, but they should not be allowed to take preeminence.
>
> Another reason I believe in the value of LSD is

due to the nature of its reputed mind-expanding properties. Men have always sought to get outside of their normalcy in one way or another; as children we enjoyed spinning in circles in order to enjoy the heady difference of dizziness. This getting outside should not be considered an escape from so-called reality or a block to effective functioning, though it can be if carried to excess. It is so easy to see everyday reality, if it exists, as an axiom. These excursions outside of reality can offer needed opportunities to see the relativity of reality, leading to a better understanding and appreciation of it. This amplification of outlook cannot help being of benefit to men.[1]

To be sure, there are people who do run into serious mental and personality problems when they use a drug like LSD. Yet I think we must honestly face the fact that a number of serious-minded people believe that there is a positive potential in regard to the mind-expanding mood drugs. According to this viewpoint, the mind-bending drugs do not provide automatic insights into reality, life, personality, religion, or the Ultimate Meaning every time one of them is popped into the mouth. The potential of the drug-induced trip is that it *might* help make the person aware of underdeveloped potential and ability that previously had been latent. The drug experience, they argue, can be a door opener to further growth and understanding. It allows new sources of insight to be tapped, and once they are, the drugs can be left behind as the search continues on new levels of relationship and personal reflection and striving.

One articulate spokesman for this view has been biochemist Robert S. DeRopp. In his book *The Master*

Game, subtitled *Pathways to Higher Consciousness Beyond the Drug Experience,* he outlines a path whereby each person can discover "a game worth playing"—the Master Game. He describes it in this manner:

> But the Master Game is played entirely in the inner world, a vast and complex territory about which men know very little. The aim of the game is true awakening, full development of the powers latent in man.[2]

The basic assumption for playing the Master Game is

> that man's ordinary state of consciousness, his so-called waking state, is not the highest level of consciousness of which he is capable.[3]

With regard to the use of the drug experience in playing this game, DeRopp argues that "it is a blind alley, a cul de sac, a dead end, nevertheless its claims must be explored." [4] Speaking more specifically, he reasons as follows:

> If they are taken under the right conditions, with proper preparation, under the supervision of one who knows how to guide the explorer in the territory he will enter, they can, on occasions at least, be of some value.[5]

And further:

> By awakening the traveler to his own inner potentialities, they provide him with a game worth playing, a task worth undertaking, a pilgrimage on which it is worthwhile to embark. . . . When he fully understands how certain effects are produced, he can learn to initiate them at will without the use of drugs.[6]

The point of all this is not to suggest that everyone should "turn on" and begin to see what it is all about. Rather, I am trying to point out that there are a significant number of persons who are attempting to use drugs to open new doors of experience in order to reach new levels of consciousness and insight. I feel that this needs to be understood because too many people condemn all drug users as "happy freaks" who want to sit around all day in a drug-induced high to contemplate their navels and escape from reality. For some, yes; but perhaps, for others, not so. At any rate if one wants to understand the use of drugs, this side of the picture must be explored. As to where it will lead—who knows at this stage of the "game"? Perhaps nowhere; nevertheless, we must ask ourselves whether this could be the unfolding of a new direction in the development of man. Up until now men have relied on Mother Nature to provide them with mood-altering potions. The laboratory creation of LSD, however, ushered in a new age of man-made mood modifiers.

The basic question, of course, is, Where do we turn for guidance and direction? It is like traveling down a new road still under construction. The signs are few and far between, and it may turn out that such drugs will be a "mindless" dead end. My own position at the moment is that I am not ready to risk my "security" to try them, but I do recognize that others are doing so for reasons that are important to them. My dilemma is centered around the indecision of following them or of trying to block the road. Since I am in nearly daily contact with people who are seeking to travel this road, it is an issue hard to avoid.

Another large area of investigation is the claim that psychedelic drugs can facilitate mystical or religious experiences. It has been clearly established that under certain conditions some persons can have profound "inner" experiences. The core of the controversy seems to center around whether or not a drug-induced experience can be truly labeled as mystical or religious. Some argue that it is all a fantasy without meaning and because of the fact that the experience is set off by a drug, it is unearned and undeserved and therefore meaningless. Others, however, maintain that the drug-induced experience represents a legitimate method of achieving mystical and religious insight upon which further growth and response can be built. Walter N. Pahnke, one of the leading researchers in this field, puts it this way:

> Many persons may not need the drug-facilitated mystical experience, but there are others who would never become aware of the undeveloped potentials within themselves or become inspired to work in this direction without such experience.[7]

The issue is certainly a large and complex one, as much hinges on what is meant by terms such as mystical and religious. To illustrate one aspect of the issue, consider the following two quotations. Both are reports of personal experiences; however, one occurred after the ingestion of a psychedelic chemical whereas the other was nonchemically induced. Which one is which? Why?

> I had the notion of "this is it—this is the moment of truth. I know that everything leads to this—complete harmony and ecstasy. . . ." We had arrived;

we were unified with the ground of being, we were already transfigured—dead, and at the same time so intensely alive as never before. I experienced a sense of initiation and participation in a great mystery—everything became knowing and known. I felt omnipotent and endowed with superhuman, divine powers.[8]

. . . till all at once, as it were out of the intensity of the consciousness of individuality, individuality itself seemed to dissolve and fade away into boundless being, and this not a confused state but the clearest, the surest of the surest, utterly beyond words—where death was an almost laughable impossibility—the loss of personality (if so it were) seeming no extinction, but the only true life. I am ashamed of my feeble description. Have I not said the state is utterly beyond words? [9]

The essence of the drug dilemma was nicely expressed by Wayne Evans at a 1967 conference on psychopharmacology:

One point we must accept. Normal people are taking psychotropic drugs now. Our task is to understand the implications of this use, both for the individual and society. . . . One must wonder if the psychopharmacology of the normal human will even become a more necessary field in the future than the psychopharmacology of the mentally ill has been in the past ten years.[10]

Evans' remarks may well turn out to be prophetic. How will we "culturize" the use of drugs? That is the question. How will we answer?

REASONS TO FAVOR OR OPPOSE

It is assumed that the use of drugs under proper medical supervision is acceptable, and that the major concern here is that of ready availability for self-prescribed use.

Reasons to Favor

1. Relief of short-term stress of anxiety, depression, or general uptightness due to the shock of death of a loved person or being in entirely new surroundings, etc.
2. Stimulation of performance; e.g., athletics, exams, job deadlines, space activities.
3. Improved mood that could enhance the willpower to diet, to improve learning patterns, or to increase creativity.
4. Gaining of new insights into one's "inner self."
5. Enhancement of mystical or religious experiences.
6. Probing into heretofore untapped levels of mood or consciousness.

Reasons to Oppose

1. Psychological dependence.
2. Physical dependence.
3. Bad trips—bummers, freakouts.
4. Personality alteration or disintegration; psychotic reactions.
5. Precipitation of antisocial behavior.
6. If pregnant, possible damage to unborn child.
7. Chromosomal changes that might lead to cancer or

other illness in the user (if damage in somatic cells) or passed on to subsequent children (if damage in germ cells).

8. Tendency toward multiple drug use.
9. Becoming a dropout dependent on society for support.

VIEWS FOR REFLECTION

The purpose of this section is to provide some statements representing the thinking of others so that the reader can reflect on them as a means of developing his own position. When an author uses only a few sentences it is inevitable that something of the overall context of his viewpoint will be lost, and in the event that damage is done to another viewpoint because of this, I apologize for my failure to understand and represent adequately the situation.

1. *What is the cause or nature of the drug problem?*

a. Adults with their alcohol and tranquilizers and students with their marihuana and LSD are both reacting to conditions which negate human values and human worth. The main difference is that the adult's drugs of choice are depressants, taken to blunt the pain. The student's drugs of choice are perceived by at least some of the more serious, rightly or wrongly, as an attempt to strike back at, to seek insight into, to protest what they feel to be the causes of the pain. It is a reasonable prediction that if all drugs were eliminated from the campus tomorrow the search would go on in some other form, perhaps more tolerable to society, perhaps less.[11]

b. Let's remember, the kids didn't invent drug abuse. *We* did. For decades now, we have bombarded the general public with the promise that any problem in life can be at least evaded, if not cured, by swallowing some kind of a pill. . . . But if you listen with both ears—you don't even need a third one—you can hardly miss the message: Problem avoidance can be managed through chemical process, and this is a good thing. Why waste sleepless hours on worry, when you can buy yourself a good night's rest for the price of a pill? [12]

c. The more we make going to school a mind-expanding experience for young people, the less likely they are to turn to a chemical. Drug use is a symptom of widespread alienation, which includes great dissatisfaction with schools which are increasingly experienced as boring and irrelevant by millions of our young people.[13]

d. In the last analysis, then, whether one chooses or not to use drugs, in full consciousness of their possible bad effects and the legal implications of drug use, becomes an existential rather than a medical decision. It is a matter of how one chooses to live one's life, how one hopes to seek experience, where and how one searches for meaning. To be sure, I doubt that we can hope to persuade students that drugs are ethically, humanly or existentially undesirable if they are not already persuaded. But I think we can at least help the student to confront the fact that in using drugs he is making a statement about how he wants to live his life.[14]

2. *What is meant by the individual's "right" to use drugs?*

a. *Do* individuals have the inalienable right, as many argue, to take any drugs they please whenever they please—especially if the drugs are nonaddictive—without interference from the law, or, for that matter, from their physicians? Should free individuals not be the sole guardians and custodians of their own inner experiences? If man chooses to sit in a room and quietly enjoy his drug-induced visions, or whatever stimulation or lethargy the drug of his choice brings him, is it anyone else's business? [15]

b. Do not be confused! The issue is not LSD. Rather it concerns your rights and responsibilities with regard to your consciousness, your soul, your internal freedom—issues not to be lost in the confusion and fear created by tabloid sociology. Your control and access to your own brain is at stake. It is not a matter to be delegated to the philosopher, theologian, or medicine man. It is our responsibility, yours and mine, and we must study and reflect upon these matters in order that our collective wisdom will determine the course of human events—a course which just might lead us to the realization of who we really are.[16]

c. To be explicit, I do not believe that we have an inalienable right to take LSD. I also believe that a person has a social responsibility, which some people tend to forget. Harming no one is fine, but what one does to oneself has reverberations well beyond oneself. One cannot resign from the human race.[17]

d. Social policy with respect to marihuana and other psychoactive drugs has many important dimensions.

. . . The most basic issue is whether or not the prohibition of behavior whose direct effects are limited to
the individual is within the function of the state.
Those who feel it is not argue that the state has no
more right to intervene with respect to the use of
harmful drugs than it does with regard to harmful
overeating. Those who take the contrary position argue that the harms are not limited to the individual
but burden society in a variety of ways; hence the
state is entitled to prohibit its use in the public interest.[18]

3. *What policy or laws should there be concerning
drugs?*

a. The prohibitive legislation now being enacted to prevent people from determining their own reactions to
psychedelics strikes at one of the most fundamental of
all liberties, the liberty of the individual to explore
his own inner world by means of his own choosing.
. . . An enlightened legislature would make such
testing possible for people who feel this need to know
more about their inner world. Instead of enacting
blanket prohibitions, they would provide proper facil-
ities under which the psychedelic experience could
be studied by any who wished to find out what it had
to offer in the way of insights and illuminations.[19]

b. Shall we then legitimatize amphetamines as well as
marihuana, on the grounds that many people like the
kick from these drugs more than they do the kick
from either alcohol or marihuana? Clearly the line
must be drawn somewhere, or else, as our pharmacological cornucopia provides us with an increasing
number of hallucinogens, euphoriants and stimulants,
we will be so burdened with intoxicants that in-

evitably we will reach a stage at which society cannot function.[20]

c. Then talk tough to your legislators. Get them to mandate ten years at hard labor for the adult pusher's first offense, and death for the second. Equate the laws covering dope peddling with those which cover premeditated poisoning. And why not? After all, cyanide and strychnine kill only the body. Dope destroys body and soul alike.[21]

d. Our present social policy toward the abuse of the dangerous drugs is wrong, perhaps disastrously wrong. We must move from our punitive policy toward a social-medical policy. A social-medical policy would not be an absolute solution for our troubles, but it would definitely cut our losses, and would therefore be a better policy, overall. As did our Prohibition policy toward the abuse of alcohol, our present posture causes more trouble than it cures. . . . A social-medical policy would simply shift to *a different set* of legal controls. Just because alcohol consumption is now legal does not mean that we do not have controls on its sale and use. The choice is not between legal controls and no controls, but between better and worse controls, between controls that have more social effectiveness and those that have less.[22]

e. Groups of men, through their governments, decide what are the acceptable limits of human behavior. There is no mandate in human experience that such decisions be logical or rational, only that they be commensurate with the majority's wishes and that they don't violate its concept of fair play. . . . But each society has its own taboos, prohibitions, and rules of conduct. These are not absolute, but relative to the attitudes of the group. . . . How society determines what should be forbidden is not a simple matter of reason. . . . The decision as to whether marihuana should be legalized is not and cannot be a black-and-white decision based on scientific fact, but rather falls within the grays of same as with alcohol.[23]

4. *Will use of one drug lead to escalation, i.e., use of other drugs?*

a. . . . escalation to other drugs? That presupposes that use of one psychoactive drug leads more or less inevitably to use of others. . . . Marijuana has no chemical or physiological effects that lead on to heroin or anything else. If widened drug use occurs—as it does, undoubtedly, with pot, as well as with alcohol, amphetamines, barbiturates and others—it is because the individual has a drug-related problem, not because of the particular drug. That calls for treatment of the individual and his ailing personality, not simply removal (even if it were possible) of one drug.[24]

b. Let's quit kidding ourselves. Marijuana is DOPE. *Cannabis sativa.* It distorts and twists and perverts. It's a facile door-opener to the hard stuff. Marijuana has the same relationship to heroin that dog-paddling has to Olympic swimming.[25]

c. Looking at drug histories, we find that most marijuana users begin with alcohol and/or tobacco as their first psycho-active drug. In terms of correlated-drug use, 99 per cent also drink, 94 per cent smoke tobacco, 50 per cent have used amphetamines, 33 per cent sedatives, 29 per cent tranquilizers, 24 per cent hallucinogens, 19 per cent special substances, and 6 per cent opiates.[26]

d. Right now the evidence is that repeated marihuana use is associated with progression to stronger drugs among a significant percentage of the marihuana users. Marihuana introduces the individual to the drug scene; if he were not so introduced the assumption is that many would never get to more powerful and dangerous agents. But marihuana is only one link in the chain that results in use of very dangerous drugs.[27]

5. *What do people expect to get from drugs, i.e., What kind of "answers" or "experiences" are they looking for?*

a. There are those who insist that pill swallowing can lead to higher consciousness. (They) are wrong. However, this much can be said in favor of the psychedelics. If they are taken under the right conditions, with proper preparation, under the supervision of one who knows how to guide the explorer in the territory he will enter, they can, on occasions at least, be of some value. They can challenge the traveler saying: "These are the mountain peaks. They really exist. Now make up your mind. Are you strong enough, persistent enough to try to climb them?" . . . They spotlight certain processes and thus make it easier for the experimentalist to recognize the mechanisms involved. When he fully understands how certain effects are produced, he can learn to initiate them at will without the use of drugs.[28]

b. As a live spirit in history, I used whatever I could to help me grow: drugs, music, love, confrontation, and the effects of all of these media mingled. With my shifts in personality went changes in my priorities. In dream, in thought, and then in action, I began to turn my energy to making a context in which I could be who I was becoming. . . . With psychedelics, into the expanded consciousness come new perceptions and connections, knowledge that transcends the mind's immediate system. We call this "mind-blowing." An order is broken. In dissonance and rich chaos, and at some depth in the bottomless water of Fear, the Self moves, from fragment to fragment, and tries to include the pieces in the harmony of a new order.[29]

c. But perhaps my basic reason for distrusting the dependence on "mind-expanding" drugs is that most people haven't learned to use the senses they possess. Speaking only for myself, I not only *hear* music; I *listen* to it when it is around, so that I find Muzak and other background music, intended to be heard but not listened to, utterly intolerable. When I am, in Carl Rogers' terms, open to my experience, I find the colors of the day, whether gray and foggy and muted or bright and sunlit, such vivid experiences that I sometimes pound my steering wheel with excitement. . . . In short, I *use* my senses—at least some of them, some of the time. And I say, why disorient your beautiful senses with drugs and poisons before you have half discovered what they can do for you? [30]

d. It is kicks, man. It is The Kick. You freak out and there is nothing but greatness and madness. If sex is your bag, you got it. If you want to see the galaxies, it's all there. If you want to iron out the wrinkles in your brain, it's the cosmic iron. Anything you want, it's there. It is the greatest flipout since the Black Mass. It's Zen and Jesus Christ and all the mad magicians rolled into one big freak. That's acid, man, and you never made the trip or you wouldn't ask.[31]

6. *What is the answer to the drug problem?*

a. Our broad objective should be to move society beyond drugs to full development of each individual's potential and to his social concern for others. The more we turn to drugs to deal with frustration, boredom, anger, and despair, the less likely we are to attack the roots of discontent and the inflexibility and unresponsiveness of our institutions and leaders. To survive and to be happy, we must transform the psychedelic ethic from *Turn on, Tune in,* and *Drop out* to: Turn on to people and the world around you; Tune in to knowledge and feeling; and Drop *in,* to improve the quality of life.[32]

b. In view of our uncertainty as to the effectiveness of drug education, it seems to me that it would be prudent to consider two disconcerting possibilities. First, that drug education may not discourage youth from experimenting with illegal drugs. Under certain circumstances, as indicated later, education may even encourage drug usage. Second, that drug education programs may be expensive and ineffective distractions which diminish our motivations to examine basic moral and political questions which may be the very roots of the drug problem.[33]

c. One of the best ways the drug experience might be developed in society is by means of the "experience center." Here would be trained psychologists and biochemists in charge of giving various drug experiences to the customers. Safety would be assured by constant physiological and psychological monitoring by computers, with rapid antidotes in readiness, to be used if necessary. To prevent abuse, only nonaddictive drugs would be used, and only a limited number of sessions per week by any one person would be permitted. The centers would provide separate enclosures for each customer, with suitable visual and auditory effects to guide and enhance a hallucinatory experience. Such experience centers would be equivalent in many ways to coffeehouses or bars; they would very likely be far more valuable, since instead of going to drown his troubles, a person could go to an experience center to understand and, hopefully, solve them.[34]

d. What to do about the dope syndrome, Mom and Pop? First, recognize it for what it is. Just one more symptom of the nation's unraveling moral fiber. A sign of our times. Then resolve to combat it in your own family, mercilessly, ceaselessly, with no holds barred. Remember that souls are the things actually at stake in the war you're declaring, and fight accordingly. Ride herd on your own kids. Know what they keep in their rooms. Know where they go when they're not home. Know who their friends are. Know what they're doing when you're not around. Don't be ashamed of interfering with your children's private lives. That's one of the things parents are for. The nation's penitentiaries are full of dead-end people whose parents were too broadminded or too indifferent to interfere with them when they were kids.[35]

QUESTIONS

In trying to take a position or find an "answer" to these questions, make an attempt to delineate the various factors that might be involved. None of these has simple answers, and it is hoped that in probing them a consistent and guiding personal ethical framework for decision will be discovered.

1. Where should the line be drawn for legal/illegal drug use? Where it is now with tobacco and alcohol legal (with controls) or should other categories of drugs be legalized, even if they are found to be harmful on the order of or less than tobacco and alcohol?

2. Would the following be a suitable alternative to the current drug laws? Every person is to be held responsible for the consequences of his action and behavior, and in the event that it impinges on the rights or behavior of others (to be defined by law—such as assault, rape, homicide, auto accidents, etc.), then that person shall be arrested and tried in a court. In other words, if one person assaults another, it would be that behavior which would be judged to be breaking the law rather than defining it on the basis of using any drug. (There are also many non-drug reasons for assaultive behavior.)

3. If the science of pharmacology develops a drug with the mood-altering potential of the "soma" of Huxley's *Brave New World*, should it be made available

to all who want it? (Soma was a drug that would "give you a holiday from the facts" by calming anger and anxiety and producing a pleasant dreamlike state.)

4. If a "safe" mood-altering drug was developed that significantly increased the chance of having a deep religious experience while participating in a service of worship, should it be allowed? If not, what are objections to drug-induced religious experience?

5. If a person wants to take a mood-altering drug, even knowing there is some possibility of a bad or psychotic reaction, should he be stopped? Why or why not? Is your answer the same for alcohol as for marijuana?

6. Should there be professionally staffed and government-licensed centers where people can go to have drug experiences under the direct supervision of trained psychologists and physicians?

7. New drugs are currently being discovered that have an aphrodisiac (sex-drive-enhancing or sex-stimulating) effect. Should these be licensed and made available by prescription only? Or totally outlawed? Two recent drugs of this kind are very simple chemicals which can be synthesized by any person knowledgeable in the arts of chemical synthesis. Therefore the possibility of a black market trade is a reality. Does this change the picture any?

8. Should appropriate mood drugs be used to control social behavior, say, tranquilizers sprayed into the air

to control a riot or stimulants used to goad troops into fighting action? What limits should be placed on the use of drugs in warfare? Some argue that it is more humane to temporarily debilitate a person rather than to kill him.

9. Many people say that they don't want to use mood drugs because they will "lose control" of themselves and become dependent on the drug for whatever happens. This is certainly consistent with the rational view of man that says we should always be in control of ourselves at all times. But could it be possible to learn from our senses and emotions through the process of "letting go"? How should we treat the sensuous side of man? Why are we sometimes afraid of our "inner world" of our minds?

10. Drugs to facilitate memory are on everyone's list for the future. But what about the opposite—amnesia or forgetting drugs? One possible use would be to allow sick or elderly persons to conserve strength for a few days while under the influence of the combination of a tranquilizer and amnesia drug. Then stimulating or psychedelic chemicals could be used to aid in recovery, if sick, or to provide novel experiences and "new life," if elderly or senile.

4

Electrical Stimulation
of the Brain

Drugs can "bend" the mind. So can electricity. In a very real sense electricity has become one of the foundation stones necessary for our modern way of life. We use it not only to simplify routine daily tasks, such as opening cans or grinding the garbage, but also to control our daily physical comfort by making our personal environments warmer or cooler. When you stop to think about it, however, there are two truly fantastic aspects to electricity: when we want it, we just flip a switch, and we don't have to understand how it is made or where it comes from in order to use it. But as we shall see in this chapter, the application of low levels of electrical power to specific sites in the brain can be a sophisticated switch for emotional and behavioral responses, as well as for simple motor reactions such as movement of the fingers. In short, the power of electricity can turn behavior on and off as readily as it does the lights.

Although the existence of electrical attraction was known to the ancient Greeks via their equivalent of the present-day schoolboy trick of running a rubber comb through his hair so that it will pick up tiny bits of paper, the ability to store and transmit electricity was not accomplished until the last half of the eighteenth century. And not surprisingly, it was not long after the discovery of methods to cause the flow of electricity, that people began to experiment with its effects on biological systems. In fact, one of the first such phenomena to be explored independently by Luigi Galvani and Alessandro Volta in the 1780's still serves today as a classical experiment in some introductory biology courses, namely, the contraction of a frog muscle when stimulated by a flow of electricity. Intriguing as this effect was, however, the electrical phenomena were studied first by physical scientists interested in the quantitative laws and relationships governing its behavior. It was not until almost a century later, in the 1870's, that concerted attention was turned to the effect of electricity on living animals. At that time it was shown that electrical stimulation of the exposed brain in anesthetized dogs could elicit localized body and limb movements.

The next big surge of interest didn't develop until the early 1920's, when Hans Berger of Austria began to measure the electrical activity of functioning brains and the Swiss physiologist W. R. Hess began to implant fine wires into the brains of cats to study the effects of electrical stimulation in awake and unanesthetized animals. Thus, Berger founded the study of electroencephalographs, called EEG for short, and Hess, likewise, the study of electrical stimulation of the brain, or ESB. The measurement of the EEG can be correlated with an individual's mental state of awareness, whereas ESB experimentation established the fact that organized motor effects and emotional reactions could be elicited from awake animals.

By the early 1950's a number of different groups were beginning to follow up these pioneering efforts with the clearly announced intention of exploring and eventually mapping the entire structure of the brain with regard to the kind of response resulting from the electrical stimulation of precise points. Even though the first studies were done with animals, it was not long until enough information and experience had been gathered to allow the selective electrical probing of damaged brains of human subjects. The intent here was to locate localized malfunctions and thereby, it was hoped, eventually to effect a cure or relief for the consequence of that damage.

Very early in these efforts with humans, Wilder Penfield discovered that this type of experimentation was opening the door to the many corridors of consciousness and activity in what many have called "the highest expression of evolution." In short, man's brain had literally been opened and experimentally contacted after some two to three million years of development. Penfield and his co-workers were concerned with a general attack on the problem of epilepsy, its origin, brain pathways of expression, and eventually its control and cure. While probing the exposed brain of epileptic patients they discovered that stimulation of certain points elicited memories that were quite specific and even sometimes recallable by repeated stimulation of the same precise point. The intriguing thing about these "memories" was that although the recollection might be of events classified as trivial, Penfield reported that "the patients have never looked upon an experiential response as a remembering. Instead of that it is a hearing-again and seeing-again—a living-through moments of past time." [1] In one case, as long as the electrical stimulation was continued, the patient actually "hummed the tune, chorus, and verse, thus accompanying the music she heard." [2] Others reported "living-memories" of events such as giving birth to a child, laughing and talking with cousins, and hearing the voice of a son playing in the yard against the ordinary background of neighborhood noises such as dogs barking, horns blowing, and other children shouting. In effect, the patients had a kind of "double consciousness" in that they were continually aware of their present experimental surroundings at the same time they perceived the electrically elicited experiences of their past. Stimulation of the visual area of the cortex similarly resulted in the sensation of bright, lighted objects, such as stars, squares, streaks, or of the opposite black forms.

It might be well to point out before going farther that, unlike the rest of our body, the brain does not have pain receptors. Therefore, there is no sensation of pain produced by either electrical probing or cutting of brain tissue (as in the famous lobotomy surgical procedures). It should also go without saying that local anesthetic procedures are used in any process that exposes the brain. During the time of electrical probing the patient is alert and able to respond to the experimenter's questioning.

By the mid-1950's rapid progress was being attained on many fronts. Space dictates that we shall have to be content with a short summarization of the highlights of the work of groups headed by Robert Heath at Tulane, James Olds at McGill, Roger Sperry at UCLA, and José Delgado at Yale. In animals (ranging from the familiar laboratory rats, cats, and monkeys to the less usual case of goats and bulls), many types of simple and complex motor responses have been evoked, such as moving of muscles or limbs. Social behavior such as aggression, dominance, and sexual mounting have also been altered. In humans, responses involved blocking of thinking processes, inhibition of speech or movement, as well as the evoking of memories, pleasure, laughter, friendliness, talking, hostility, fear, and hallucinations. Additional details on some of these responses will be given shortly.

The Technique:
How It Is Done

Even though a functioning brain is a complex array of some ten billion interconnected neurons, the basic operating mechanism is an electrochemical one. This means that the firing of the neurons, and thus the appearance of a response such as muscle movement or the feeling of an emotion, can be triggered by electrical or chemical influences in the appropriate area. And even though large numbers of neurons are necessary for the production of any given behavioral response, it turns out that it is not necessary to stimulate simultaneously all the necessary neurons. In other words, stimulation at appropriate locations along a particular pathway of interconnected neurons is all that is necessary to elicit a given response. If this were not true, then the process of ESB would undoubtedly be so complex as to preclude any meaningful use of the technique.

The technique for electrical stimulation of the brain involves the process of surgically implanting thin wire electrodes into the brain so that by the simple process of switching an electric current on or off, an experimenter can control the stimulation of neurons in a specific area of an awake and mobile animal or human. These electrodes are insulated except for the tip, thereby not only ensuring a very precise and localized presentation of electricity, but also making it possible to group a number of wires of different lengths into a bundle allowing for controlled stimulation of different depths in the brain tissue.

In the early work the implanted electrodes were attached to a multiple socket which was in turn fastened to the skull. For experimental hook-up, then, additional external wires were necessary for attachment to the electrical controls. Obviously, such an arrangement affects the mobility of an experimental animal (in spite of some ingenious swivel arrangements), so eventually methods were developed that allowed for the attachment of the brain electrodes to a miniature radio receiver which was in turn attached to the animal. Thus electrical stimulation could be accomplished by sending a radio signal to the brain electrodes while the animal had complete freedom of movement. Experimental designs have also incorporated the aspect of self-stimulation: in animals, resulting from the pressing of a lever, and in humans, from simply pressing a button on a miniature radio device attached to the belt. In this way it is possible to investigate the rewarding or unrewarding nature of a given stimulation by allowing for a means whereby the subject can control the number and frequency of the stimulations.

Recent sophisticated equipment developed by Delgado has reached the level of two-way radio communicators, called stimoceivers. This procedure allows for radio transmission and reception of electrical messages to and from the brain. One example of the utility of this method is signal communication between the brain of a monkey and a computer. Although these studies are in the early stages, it is already clear that it is possible to monitor unconscious activity of the brain so that when certain predetermined signals are noted by the computer, it can respond by automatically signaling electrical stimulation in another preselected site in the brain.

By way of summary, we can note three important factors in the success of the ESB technique: electrodes are well tolerated for long periods of time (years) and do not affect normal behavior when unstimulated; although some local damage is done in the process of implanting the electrodes, it has not proven to be serious; and multiple numbers of electrodes can be implanted at desirable depths and in precise locations without open brain surgery. Also, without going into detail, it should be pointed out that the technique of ESB requires great skill, not only surgically, but also electronically. At this juncture the technique is quite a sophisticated one and is by no means to be considered a routine procedure for general use (except in the hands of a small group of researchers).

WHAT IS POSSIBLE TODAY?

It would be quite easy to fill a large book with descriptions of the many different kinds of experimental situations and responses encountered with the ESB technique. For our purposes, however, it will suffice to consider a few examples from the work of different investigators to get some sort of feel for the large variety of existing pos-

sibilities. Since our concern is mainly with the modifica-
tion of behavior, no attempt will be made to correlate
responses with particular locations in the brain; in some
cases, stimulation will be discussed without identifying a
specific site.

ANIMAL STUDIES

1. *Simple motor response.*[3] The bending (flexion) of a
leg of a cat can be induced by stimulation of the proper
point in the motor cortex. How much the leg moves depends on the applied intensity of the electrical signal.
If the normal intensity needed to bend the leg is applied
while the cat is in the air (say in the process of jumping
off a table), the bending response does not occur. On the
other hand, if the magnitude of the stimulus is increased,
it is possible to cause bending of the leg while the cat is
in midair. The result is, of course, an abnormal three-
point landing for the cat. This is one example of many,
that shows that the ESB response can be made to be
stronger than normal behavior control induced by the
environment or normal activity.

2. *Complex motor response.*[4] The sequence of events
listed below always took place in the same order following
a five-second stimulation of the red nucleus in a monkey's brain. Even though considerable flexibility was
noted in the details of the responses, the sequence was so
reliable that it persisted after 20,000 stimulations!

Sequence: [5] "(1) immediate interruption of spontaneous activity; (2) change in facial expression; (3) turning
of the head to the right; (4) standing on two feet; (5)
circling to the right; (6) walking on two feet with perfect

balance, using both arms to maintain equilibrium during bipedestation; (7) climbing a pole; (8) descending to the floor; (9) uttering a growl; (10) threatening and often attacking and biting a subordinate monkey; (11) changing aggressive attitude and approaching the rest of the group in a friendly manner; (12) resuming peaceful spontaneous behavior."

3. *Eating inhibition.*[6] A cat can be immobilized with its tongue out while in the process of lapping milk. In another situation a monkey was stimulated with its mouth full of banana; the response was cessation of chewing, emptying of the mouth, and throwing away of the banana.

4. *Thirst.*[7] A 10–20-second stimulation in goats caused drinking behavior which lasted for two to three seconds after the stimulation ceased. It was possible by repeated stimulation to cause the body weight to be increased by 40 percent as a result of drinking water. In another situation one goat drank 16 liters (about 4 gallons) of water in a period of five hours.

5. *Aggression.*[8] Cerebral stimulation in a charging bull was able to inhibit the aggressive behavior so that in mid-charge the bull stopped abruptly and turned aside. Although surely not as significant, it must be of some import that another point was stimulated 100 times with the result of 100 consecutive moos!

6. *Pleasure center.*[9] One of the early discoveries was the presence of what is popularly called a pleasure center. It may be that instead of actual pleasure sensations, stimulation of this center sets up a reverberating and

uncontrollable behavioral response which causes the animal to seek continued self-stimulation. Another way of looking at it has been to assume that the stimulation apparently produced such intense pleasure or reward that the subject greatly desired continual stimulation. In situations with self-stimulation levers, rats have been known to push the lever at an astonishing rate of 5,000 times per hour. Attempts to satisfy the rat's appetite for this reward have lasted over twenty-four consecutive hours. Only physical fatigue and exhaustion would cause the rat to cease the self-stimulation. In experiments comparing the desire for this reward with that for food, it was determined that rats would cross an electrified floor (they detest shocks on their feet) to reach the pleasure self-stimulation bar, while rats starved twenty-four hours for food would not cross such a barrier to get to food. In fact, starving rats, given the choice between food and brain rewards, choose the brain rewards.

7. *Maternal affection*.[10] In one experiment a ten-second stimulation caused a female monkey to abandon her youngster and assume aggressive attitudes for eight to ten minutes, ignoring completely her baby's calls for attention.

8. *Complex social behavior*.[11] Ali, the chief of a small monkey colony, normally showed his dominant role by a show of ill temper (biting his own hand) and by threatening others. However, with the ESB technique it was possible to block his aggressiveness and prevent him from attempting to attack another member of the colony. A lever was placed in the cage with the colony, such that when it was pressed a five-second stimulation of Ali's

brain reduced his agressiveness. After some random lever-pressing by the colony members, Elsa, a female, discovered what pressing the lever would do. From that time on whenever Ali would threaten her, she would press the lever and look him straight in the eye (something just not done by a submissive monkey, unless he was looking for trouble). Elsa did not become the dominant monkey in the colony, but she did block Ali's aggressiveness to some extent and helped maintain a peaceful coexistence within the whole colony.

HUMANS

1. *Motor effect.*[12] ESB can stimulate the closing of the hand into a fist. The sensation has been reported as not being unpleasant, and even when warned that the stimulation was coming, the closing of the hand could not be prevented. In an unwarned situation, stimulation while turning the page of a magazine resulted in the crumpling and tearing of the page as the subject's hand was closed into a fist.

2. *Pleasure center.*[13] A cooperative and intelligent thirty-year-old female had suffered from psychomotor and grand mal attacks; however, normal behavior was observed as being reserved and poised. Stimulation of her "pleasure center" in the amygdala area produced a pleasant sensation of relaxation and elicited an increased and more intimate verbal and emotional output toward the therapist, who was new to her. This kind of behavior was not noted with stimulations of other areas, although the behavior noted above could be repeated with the

appropriate stimulation. In a male patient an area was found which produced a highly rewarding and pleasurable sensation described as "feeling good" and which built up to, but did not reach, a feeling of sexual orgasm.

3. *Rage.*[14] A woman with a history of frequent and unpredictable occurrences of rage and physical assault was committed to a ward for the criminally insane. Electrodes were implanted in an attempt to explore for possible neurological abnormalities, and at one point in the studies, a particular area in the amygdala was stimulated while she was playing the guitar and singing. Seven seconds after the stimulation, a fit of rage and anger was precipitated in which she threw away the guitar and attacked the wall. After a few minutes of pacing around the floor in an agitated state, she gradually quieted down and resumed her usual cheerful behavior. Subsequent stimulation showed that this general rage response could be repeated.

4. *Self-stimulation.*[15] Electrodes in fourteen different brain regions were implanted in a man suffering from narcolepsy (an uncontrollable desire to sleep). Exploration of the responses turned up one area which had the effect of increasing alertness but which was accompanied by a corresponding increase in feelings of discomfort. Because one area was found which could control the symptoms of the narcolepsy, the patient was fitted with a device for self-stimulation so that when he began to feel sleepy during the day he could press the button and stimulate his brain to keep him awake. Wearing this device allowed him to return to part-time employment. His

friends and fellow patients soon learned, however, that if he did fall asleep before being able to stimulate himself, they could awaken him by pressing the button for him!

In another patient, fifty-one electrode leads were implanted into brain sites with the following kinds of subjective responses: feeling great, elimination of bad thoughts, feeling drunk (his "happy button"), feeling sick, and no response at all. With regard to the rewarding sites, the patient self-stimulated at rates up to nearly 500 times per hour.

Clinical Uses

The first twenty years of ESB exploration has already uncovered numerous situations having clinical and therapeutic importance in humans. When this is coupled with the fact that the mapping of specific areas in the brain is still in its infancy, it seems reasonable to assume that a wealth of information about subtle and sophisticated, as well as powerful, behavioral applications is on the foreseeable horizon. However, for the purposes of our limited discussion, we shall mention only a few possibilities in two general areas: diagnostic and therapeutic treatment and brain-computer communication. We have come a long way in recent years in terms of psychotherapy and the use of psychoactive drugs in controlling the problems of psychosis, epilepsy, Parkinson's tremors, and episodes of intolerable pain. This progress will no doubt continue. Nevertheless, the precise character of the ESB process holds much promise not only for the gross control of these conditions but also possibly in regard to the fine-tuning of everyday mental operations.

In short, the dramatic progress of the past two decades is really only the first few faltering steps in our exploration of the corridors of consciousness.

1. *Diagnostic and therapeutic opportunities.*[16] No doubt most of us have encountered the ECG (electrocardiogram) procedure in which a recording of the electrical activity of the heart muscle provides a trained doctor with the information necessary to diagnose the presence of a particular heart problem, or in happy cases to declare the situation normal. As we saw early in this chapter, the same thing can be done with the measurement of the spontaneous electrical activity of the brain, called EEG (electroencephalograph) in this case. However, the sophistication of the art of diagnosis here is limited seriously by the fact that the EEG measurement gets information by means of surface electrodes which are insulated from the inner structures of the brain by the skull, intracranial fluid, and various tissues. Also when one keeps in mind that unlike the simple heart muscle, which is basically a pump, the brain is a fantastically complex collection of ten billion or so highly interconnected neurons, it is intuitively clear that the correlation of behavioral or disease syndromes with specific sites in the brain is a very tall order indeed for the interpretation of EEG information. By contrast, though, the ESB method provides for a depth probe into selected and specific sites which might be implicated in the production of certain types of abnormal behavior. For example, Parkinson's disease is characterized by continuous involuntary movements of the muscles. In some

cases by probing the brain electrically it is possible to block certain neuronal discharges which are causing the involuntary movements. So as a diagnostic procedure, a specific area of the brain might be located as the "trouble" source, and then decisions can be made as to the viability and desirability of treatment either by freezing the cerebral tissues in the area (and thus damaging them) or by rendering them inactive by electrical coagulation—using a large current of electricity to cause the permanent neuronal damage.

This type of stereotactic surgery (i.e., being specific in that destruction of brain tissue occurs only in a limited spatial area) has many advantages over the more traditional surgical methods known popularly as lobotomy which reached a height of popularity in the late 1940's and early 1950's. In that procedure large areas of the temporal lobes of the brain were removed or their connections with other areas of the brain severed by use of a scalpel. The stereotactic surgical method requires much less of an opening in the surface of the brain, it destroys less than one tenth as much brain tissue, and it is generally a surer procedure since the electrodes can determine if the area to be destroyed is in fact the one causing or contributing to the undesirable behavior.

Recall the situation mentioned earlier of the woman who had a history of unprovoked assaults. This woman had had extensive medical care and years of psychotherapy in an effort to control her assaultive behavior—all to no avail. However, by the use of ESB probes it was possible to locate precisely an area in the brain that, when stimulated, could "artificially" produce the rage type of behavior. This clinical information was enough to guide her doctors in the proper placement of a therapeutic lesion in her brain. She has suffered from only two mild rage episodes in the two years following the operation.

A second brief case history can illustrate more dramatically the same general point.[17] Clara T. was a sixty-two-year-old woman with a twenty-nine-year history of grand mal and temporal lobe epileptic seizures which began after a fall on ice. Because of an increase in the frequency of the seizures, a lobectomy was performed in which part of her left temporal lobe was surgically removed (known as frontal lobe lobotomy). The seizures decreased for four months, but then Clara began to lose her memory and to assault physically almost anyone who came near. One evening it took four nurses and two male orderlies forty-five minutes to repel her violent behavior and to control this eighty-six-pound woman! ESB probing in her right temporal lobe showed that malfunctioning there was causing this assaultive behavior, but because it was known that the surgical removal of this other temporal lobe would effectively remove all chance for recovery, another lobectomy was out of the question. However, via electric coagulation in a localized area of the right temporal lobe, her condition was stabilized to the point that six years after the operation she was having fewer epileptic seizures, had had no rage or unprovoked assaults, and was able to return home.

The combined clinical and therapeutic use of the ESB technique has spread to many medical centers throughout the world, so that hundreds of patients with various kinds of mental defects have been treated. We shall attempt here to point out the results with only two groups of patients in two different treatment centers.[18] In one group of 13 epileptics, H. Narabayashi in Japan reported that 4 were dramatically improved, 3 improved initially, but relapsed in six to twelve months, and 6 were not improved. However, in a group of 27 children with mentally defective assaultive behavior, 14 showed dramatic improvement, 9 significant improvement, and 4 no improvement. Professor R. R. Heimberger, of the University of Indiana, has reported that in a group of 25 severely epileptic patients, the behavioral abnormality was eliminated in 7, convulsions eliminated in 4 and improved (i.e., lessened frequency) in 12 and an overall improvement in 23, 2 of whom were subsequently released from the hospital.

In general, then, although we are not talking about a panacea for all mental illness, it is quite clear that the ESB procedure can provide a doctor with a very specialized and specific tool for locating areas in the brain, the blockage or stimulation of which might result in the relief of intolerable pain, assaultive behavior, epileptic seizures, or abnormal hyperkinetic movements. Of course, it must be remembered that because of the vast complexity of the brain, initial diagnostic work requires a great deal of skill and is by nature purely empirical and in part, dependent upon chance observation of desirable effects. Even knowing what area to look in, investigators are still confronted with a needle-in-the-haystack proposition. But they *are* finding the needles!

2. *Brain-computer communication.* The development by Delgado of the miniature two-way radio devices called stimoceivers opened the doors to some genuinely

new aspects of experience and communication in that they provide a method for a new kind of feedback exchange of information between a living brain and a machine. One such experiment can illustrate the basic elements in this method.[19]

In an experiment carried out by Delgado a chimpanzee was equipped with a stimoceiver which could relay the brain activity of the right and left amygdaloid nuclei to a computer for automatic recording and analysis. The computer was programmed to recognize a specific pattern of electrical activity, called spindling, which had previously been shown to be normally present in both amygdaloid nuclei for periods of about one second several times per minute. At the receipt of this spindling signal, the computer was programmed to automatically send radio signals to another area of the brain in the reticular formation. Stimulation of this area had previously been determined to have the ability to reduce that activity. The result was that within two hours of the beginning of this two-way feedback communication, the spindling activity was reduced to only half its normal level; and six days later, with daily two-hour periods of computer feedback, the spindle activity was reduced to only one percent of normal. When the computer linkage was disconnected, the spindling returned to normal within two weeks. The whole sequence could then be repeated in a reproducible manner.

Another area of investigation has been that of using computer signals to replace signals normally sent from one area of the brain to another. Damage to the cortex area of the brain is sometimes of the type that a communication pathway inside the brain is disrupted. For example, even though the motor areas in the brain for causing the movement of a limb might be intact, if the area responsible for translating the thought "I want to move my arm" into an action signal to that motor area is not functioning, it would not be possible for me to move my arm. Working with monkeys, Lawrence Pinneo, of the Stanford Research Institute, has developed a technique whereby a computer can send a signal to the motor area for limb movement in place of the "I want to" signal from a damaged area.[20] The result is that simple movements of previously disabled limbs have been achieved. The obvious hope for human use is that the disabling effects of strokes and certain brain injuries can be overcome by bypassing the damaged area of the brain.

These experiments clearly establish the entrance of a new medical tool, namely, electrical therapeutic feedback between a living brain and a computer. We can readily imagine a scenario for the control of a condition such as epilepsy. When a certain type of brain activity begins which is known to precede the epileptic seizure, the information could be automatically radio-relayed to a computer which could then signal the brain to inhibit that activity, provided of course, that such an inhibitory area exists. By such a process it might be possible to avoid epileptic seizures without the patient ever being aware of their possible onset. Or in the situation where some type of recognizable premonition or feeling precedes the onset of a seizure, it might be possible for a person to push a button and then by self-stimulation abort the oncoming seizure.

LIMITATIONS

As we have seen, ESB can activate and influence a rather diverse pattern of behavior in animals and humans, and although it is always dangerous to say that something can't be done, there do seem to be some clearly understood limitations to this technique. Nevertheless, one can hedge one's bets a little by pointing out that the limitations described are the result of the present state of the knowledge and are always subject to change as new knowledge is gained.

1. *Robot behavior.* It is not possible to electrically synthesize and control the individual components of a complex motor performance such as opening a door or driving a car. ESB is a type of nonspecific stimulus in which there is no feedback from the environment. In other words, all it can do is continue to activate the same group of neurons without any chance of establishing or changing a sequence of responses which would result from an adaptation to the environment. However, even though it is not possible to synthesize each component of a complex motor performance, it has been demonstrated in numerous situations that it is possible to provide the motivation to press a lever or open a door. The point is simply that movements cannot be controlled like a robot, i.e., turn right here, open the door there, etc. Recall the complex sequence of events evoked in a monkey which persisted in the same order for 20,000 stimulations. Some might term this a kind of robot behavior, but again the

point is that it is not possible to break into that chain of events and substitute an additional movement.

2. *New skills*. It is not possible to create electrically a skill that is not already present, such as using a type-writer, speaking an unknown language, or solving problems. ESB is a method for stimulating specific neurons and is not a process for creating newly coordinated sensory pathways in the brain which would in effect represent a new skill. Another way of saying this is that ESB cannot evoke anything that is not already in the brain; new neuronal connections are not created by the electrical impulse.

3. *Predictability*. It is not possible to predict beforehand what the response will be to the initial stimulation of a specific area in the brain. In some areas no responses are noted, in terms of either subjective feeling or a change in behavior.

4. *Personality*. It has not yet been possible via ESB to create a new personality in an individual because it can only stimulate what is already in the brain, i.e., each person responds on the basis of his personal experience and background. However, the true extent of this "limitation" is not yet clear, since as we have seen it is possible to make a person friendlier, to precipitate a condition of rage, or to influence his train of thought.

5. *Technical complexity*. Considerable skill and knowledge is necessary in order to place an electrode properly. For this reason, it does not appear likely that clandestine outfits for ESB control will be sold or used. The possibility does exist, though.

SUMMARY

The physical control of many kinds of animal and human mental functions is now a demonstrated and well-established fact. It is possible to evoke, maintain, modify, or inhibit a wide variety of responses whether they be classified as emotional, individual, or social behavior. The clinical applications of these techniques are truly astounding in their scope. Man has always attempted to control his fellowman and to gain a greater measure of self-control. Yet the prospects of being able to do either with a set of fine wires and a switch has placed a new element into this age-old contest. And even before we can have a chance to get used to this, the marvels of the computer are being plugged into the system. We should never forget that it is a man who programs the computer and tells it what to do. Still, the prospect of controlling the brain with a machine is one that will take a lot of getting used to.

5

Plugged-In Behavior

"Switching on" may replace "turning on" as the symbol of a future generation. Man has always searched for the twins of satisfaction and significance, whether it be in climbing the highest mountain peaks or in probing the depths of a meditative trance. Neither activity comes easily. Each requires lengthy and arduous preparation. Not so, however, with ESB. Granting that sophisticated knowledge and intensive training are needed to master the techniques for implanting electrodes does not take away from the fact that to experience the results of the technique requires nothing but the possession of a living brain. Who can doubt that we are face-to-face with a new quality of experience? Who can predict what doors will open as man explores the corridors of consciousness?

One way of looking at human behavior is to recognize that it is the expression of a functioning brain. That is to say, all the infinite varieties and responses and relationships that we call behavior result from the concert of electrochemical responses of millions upon millions of individual but highly interrelated cells. But this is said not to sully man's image and reduce all of his complex behavior to a multitude of electrochemical switches or equations. The story of the evolution of man's brain with its unique development of a cortical outer layer allowing for the phenomenon of self-recognition is a fascinating one that even in its broad outlines portrays the incredible drive for complexity that seems to be inherent in the movement of evolution through time. Yet as we deliberate about the sociopolitical, legal, moral, and religious framework of man's relationship to his fellowman, we often ignore the fact that one half of the equation of human behavior, whether violent or peaceful, whether loving or despicable, whether climbing a tree or sleeping, is the presence of a functioning brain. Living, and thus behavior, is a product of a *brain-environment* interaction.

Much of the time I think we could argue that discussion of man's behavior is really not much more than a response to and focus on what he is doing or has done, i.e., observation of his activity. Even though we give lip service to the environment, our current eco-awareness is a blunt reminder of the fact that in our rush to live we have sorely neglected to consider the impact of our activity on the physical environment. But also if we really look closely at ourselves, we should clearly recognize that the psychological and sociological aspects of our environment are also just as sorely neglected—witness the sensory impact of blocks upon blocks of blazing neon signs, the numerous inane and insipid television commercials, and the up-tightness of the silent majority in America as they are buffeted by civil rights and antiwar protest movements, drugs, long hair, and loud music. Our environment, both physical and psychological, is trying to tell us something; but so far we have shown an amazing tendency to see through darkly shaded glasses and thus dull the input to our behavior center, the brain. Yet, the ability to express these problems shows that they are recognizable. The role of the brain, nevertheless, receives nearly zero attention. Perhaps because it is so obviously a part of us, i.e., without it we would have no consciousness, that we can so blithely ignore it. But if even a fraction of the implications of present-day brain research come to pass, we are going to be forced to give serious attention to the brain half of the brain-environment interaction, or in short, behavior.

In broad terms, and from the point of view of the brain, behavior depends upon five factors: (1) its physical structure, (2) the biochemical and electrical functioning of that structure, (3) the information stored from past experience, (4) the information being received from the "outside" or current experience, and (5) the association made between the present and past information. The first two, physical structure and biochemical-electrical functioning, are genetically given, but changes in them can be made via disease or accidental injury. To date much of the thrust of brain research has been aimed toward understanding and manipulating these two functions. Indeed, the major goal of these kinds of efforts is someday to deduce a physical-biochemical theory to explain the multitude of behaviors lumped under the rubric of "mental illness." On the other hand, modern science is not ignoring the other three factors pertaining to information storage, retrieval, and association of our experience. A broad and integrative understanding here will have wide-range impacts on our concepts of intelligence.

It is estimated that more than ten million Americans

suffer from some obvious brain damage: one half million from cerebral palsy, two million from convulsive disorders, two and one half million from hyperkinetic-behavior disorders, and six million from mental retardation. And another five million have brains that are subtly damaged and not functioning properly. Stated in another way, somewhere between 5 and 10 percent of our population have brains that are not functioning in a "normal" way. The question, then, is simply, How seriously do we take this in terms of our relationship to criminals in prison and to our children in schools? to suggest two examples. Don't read this to mean that I am implying that 10 percent of our population is "crazy" and that we should do something to weed them out. I am trying to get us to wrestle with the significance of a large factor generally ignored in society improvement discussions, namely, the presence of abnormally functioning brains.

We have ignored the question of how the brain has developed, for that is a subject far beyond the scope of this limited effort. However, considerable public interest has been generated lately by ethologists as they have attempted to understand man's behavior in relation to his evolutionary ties to the animal kingdom, e.g., Desmond Morris' *The Naked Ape*, Konrad Lorenz's *On Aggression*, and Robert Ardrey's *The Territorial Imperative*. With regard to violent behavior many ethologists argue from two basic points: man has an inherited aggressive instinct and cerebral control mechanisms have not been evolved that would prevent this instinct from dominating behavior in certain situations. That is to say, man is an aggressive creature by nature, and there is nothing he can do about his susceptibility to violent behavior. However, this view has been challenged by two brain researchers, Vernon H. Mark and Frank R. Ervin, in their recent book *Violence and the Brain*.[1] In outline, their argument begins with the acceptance of the fact that violence is a potential behavior which has a long evolutionary history measured in hundreds of millions of years. "Any animal, regardless of its species, reacts to a life threatening attack with one of two patterns of behavior: either with flight, or with aggression and violence —that is, fight."[2]

They base their alternate view on three contentions. First, aggression is not a simple instinct but is "one of a number of different varieties of behavior which are controlled and modulated at different levels of brain function."[3] So even though there is a basic fight or flight brain mechanism, the patterns of its use in aggressive violence against other men are learned responses which result from interaction with the environment. Second, ESB probing demonstrates that "powerful cerebral mechanisms do exist which in extreme cases can stop directed attack behavior in midcharge."[4] And third, brain disease or malfunction can override this control. The impact and direction of this line of reasoning, then, is that "individual violence may be one of the symptoms of a disturbance in the brain mechanisms that control, initiate, and suppress violent behavior."[5] More pointedly, Mark and Ervin are suggesting by this argument that if we are really to deal with the problems of violence in our society, we are going to have to combine the efforts of sociological professionals with those of brain scientists and clinicians.

Yearly violence levels in our society are of the following magnitude: 14,000 murders, 31,000 rapes, 288,000 aggravated assaults on adults and one million on infants and children, and 60,000 deaths and three million injuries from auto accidents. In view of the fact that the best efforts of numerous social psychologists, educators, etc., have not been able to stem this tide, Mark and Ervin ask:

> Can this violence ever be controlled by the kind of environmental manipulation now being used even if it were done well, or is some additional approach worth trying? [6]

> The present methods—which depend upon changing only environmental factors—have proved inadequate; and, in persons whose violence is related to brain dysfunction, they will continue to be inadequate.[7]

I once heard a New York legislator say that some people are just basically bad and dangerous and that the only way to protect society from them was to lock them up. I readily admit that I have never seen or known one of these inherently violent criminals, but I do think we should take pause to examine the human impact of such a viewpoint, which effectively says that nothing can be done, and thus offers the possibility of leading to a dead-end street for a human life. If it is true that acts we define as criminal (murder, rape, assault) might be the result of a malfunctioning brain, the question immediately arises whether society should make an attempt at rehabilitation via brain surgery of some type. Right from the beginning one runs into the question of whether anyone has the right to tamper in a surgical way with the brain of another person. The first impulse is to say, "No." But further reflection brings forth the realization that the very act of imprisonment also has a profound impact on that same brain. If one of the purposes of a prison is to provide for rehabilitation, should we not make available surgical treatment for those with a long history of assault and criminal behavior? Would not the correcting of a brain dysfunction re-create the possibility for a new chance for life? This kind of suggestion is not meant to be a routine panacea for an ESB solution to prison overpopulation. Rather, the question is, To what extent should we use our knowledge of the brain to alter or influence the brain half of the brain-environment view of behavior?

Psychoactive drugs and psychotherapy are powerful tools for the treatment of mental illness, but more sophisticated knowledge of the brain could put us on the threshold of being able to "tune" an individual's behavior to fit between the limits of some norm. One general theory of mental illness is that the abnormal behavior is a result of the formation of new habits of thought which in some manner bypass or suppress older ones. Because these new habits must involve new pathways of interconnection among the neurons in the brain, the thought is that if one could alter, disrupt, or even erase these new habits, then the old ones could be re-established or the person put in a position to learn new and "healthy" patterns.

But there is a problem (ignoring the rather formidable one of devising an electrical method to alter neuronal pathways) that stems from our understanding of the brain which tells us that the highest intellectual and emotional processes are in effect controlled by the same kind of neuronal pathways that regulate muscular behavior. So the question is, How far should we go toward attempting to alter electrically neuronal pathways in the brain? Do we really want to "cure" mental illness? Indeed, what, after all, *is* mental illness? Are there not tensions resembling schizophrenic behavior that are basic to the process of creativity? Without extending the discussion, consider how one author puts it:

> It is even possible that some of our great art, literature, and religion owes its inspiration to the uncontrolled electric discharge of small regions of damaged tissue in the brains of creative people! [8]

One specter still looms in the foreground—the ability to control completely another person's brain against his will. It cannot be avoided, the potential is there. How we will respond to this threat is a scenario we may see acted out before our eyes in the next few decades. Man has always tried to control the minds of others, either singly or in groups, and the list of methods tried would probably be endless. The ESB technique is by its nature a personal one—everyone "controlled" has to be implanted. Yet in the light of the fact that most of us are followers and only a few are leaders, it might be possible to exhibit a large measure of overall control by using only a handful of controllees. It is a sad but inevitable truth that our knowledge always comes as a two-edged sword. To have the promise of relief of mental illness, one must also accept, with the other hand, the threat of the control of the brain by someone else. But even the fact that man has yet to solve this dilemma is not enough to signal a halt to his activities. Man goes on.

REASONS TO FAVOR OR OPPOSE

Reasons to Favor

1. Control or cure antisocial behavior that results from malfunctioning of brain by locating the trouble spot via ESB and then destroying malfunctioning neurons with a larger jolt of electricity.

2. Allow for fine-tuning of mood and thus reduce anxiety, depression, and perhaps neuroses.

3. Control of severe types of mental illness: schizophrenia, psychoses, etc.

4. Control of diseases resulting from brain malfunction: Parkinson's disease, epileptic seizures, etc.

5. Perhaps discover and open up new channels of creativity and consciousness via stimulation of combinations of different brain areas.

6. Possible control of memory through erasure or implantation.

Reasons to Oppose

1. Potential for a dictator to control subjects by using brain stimulation for pain or mental discomfort as a threat or stimulation of pleasure or sexual orgasm as a reward.

2. Creation of "electric-heads" who would get wired up for pleasure and become society dropouts dependent on others for support.

3. Potential for psychological disturbance as a result of long-term use of ESB.

Views for Reflection

1. *Why should we study the brain?*

a. Perhaps it is time to ask if the present orientation of our civilization is desirable and sound, or whether we should re-examine the universal goals of mankind and pay more attention to the primary objective, which should not be the development of machines, but of man himself.[9]

b. The human race is at an evolutionary turning point. We're very close to having the power to construct our own mental functions, through a knowledge of genetics (which I think will be complete within the next 25 years); and through a knowledge of the cerebral mechanisms which underlie our behavior. The question is what sort of humans would we like, ideally, to construct? Not only our cities are very badly planned; we as human beings are, too. The results in both cases are disastrous.[10]

c. Man once used his intelligence to achieve ecological liberation, so that he no longer had to be wet when it rained, or cold when the sun was hidden, or killed because predators were hungry. He can achieve mental liberation also. Through an understanding of the brain, the brain itself may act to reshape its own structures and functions intelligently. That we bring this about is most essential for the future of mankind.[11]

d. If we could modify mental mechanisms intelligently, the consequences would be far more important than the consequences of extending man's life span or limiting his birth rate, because to influence mental processes is to influence the source of all human activities.[12]

e. What then is the actual localization of function in the brain? What are the strings that must be pulled to make that superpuppet, man, dance in whichever way desired? Let me emphasize the importance of the answer to this question; it will tell us exactly how to control our own behavior and that of others. This knowledge is the most important that man can ever find out about himself.[13]

2. *In what ways should we attempt to apply the techniques of ESB?*

a. Brain surgery is fortunately not the means of curbing aggression, but it is a valuable method to have in reserve when others fail. Even when violent dispositions are not the result of brain damage, implantation may still be used to cope with it and may be the kindest way of doing so. If the unusual distribution of male sex chromosomes called "XYY," for example, should turn out reliably to predict a genetic disposition to violence, as some scientists think it might, implantation might be more desirable than jail, . . . since there is no evident way to remove a person's chromosomes and start him over. But since surgery is the least reversible of known coercive methods, the question will always remain as to whether it is justified simply because it is the most efficient.[14]

b. Suppose . . . he is sent—not off to jail, but into the hospital for brain surgery. The surgeon delicately readjusts the distorted amygdala, and the criminal has now become a gentle soul with a sweet, loving disposition. He would not do violence to a flea. He is shocked to hear of the kind of crimes his former self had commited. The man is clearly a stranger to the man who was wheeled into the operating room. *Is* he the same man, really? Is he responsible for the crimes that he—or that other person—committed? Can he be punished? Should he go free? [15]

c. One of the implications of this study is that unwanted patterns of brain activity—for instance those correlated with assaultive or antisocial activity—could be recognized by the computer before they ever reached consciousness in order to trigger pacification of the subject. Another speculation is that the onset of epileptic attacks could be recognized and avoided by feedback.[16]

d. If he can really learn to control his own emotions, man will veritably be able to bring himself to life. The director in charge of an actor wired for emotions will be able to bring him to life under his control. Indeed, the enlargement of experience by means of pulling the emotional strings harder than can be done naturally may well allow the ultimate of possible human experiences. Man will be able fully to explore his potentialities when such control of the emotions becomes possible.[17]

e. There exists even now a very interesting possibility of two human beings having electrodes placed in their sexual reward centers, each transmitting by short-wave radio to the other the intensity of his or her excitement and level of reward, so that it stimulates the other's electrodes. The lovemaking of such a couple would be explosive and extremely satisfying; there would certainly be a meeting of minds as well as bodies when that occurred! [18]

Also in regard to electrodes in sexual reward centers.

f. And in a permissive society, where there is a great deal of changing of sexual companions, the most favored would be those with enhanced powers. They would be the flames around which the moths would dance. But more people would want to be the favored flames with their sexual powers burning brightly; such treatment would most likely spread very rapidly. It is even possible to envisage such a movement getting out of hand; a far greater amount of time would be spent on sexual intercourse, possibly bringing other activities to a halt. But since there is expected to be more leisure in the automated society of the future, what better way of spending it than in sexual ecstacy! [19]

3. *What are the prospects for control of behavior by using ESB?*

a. The notion of a man controlling his own brain is one thing. But the prospect that a man's brain might be controlled by another man is something else again—not to mention the control of masses of people by a few powerful individuals. . . . The fact that it might be difficult or troublesome (and it could soon become less difficult and less troublesome) to apply ESB on a large scale would not necessarily deter someone who was sufficiently motivated to do it, and had the power to carry out his will. . . . It has been suggested that a dictator might even implant electrodes in the brains of infants a few months after birth—and they would never know that their thoughts, moods, feelings, and all-around behavior were not the results of their own volition. Where then is free will, and individual responsibility? [20]

b. Could a ruthless dictator stand at a master radio transmitter and stimulate the depth of the brains of a mass of hopelessly enslaved people? This Orwellian possibility may provide a good plot for a novel, but fortunately it is beyond the theoretical and practical limits of ESB. By means of ESB we cannot substitute one personality for another, nor can we make a behaving robot of a human being. It is true that we can influence emotional reactivity and perhaps make a patient more aggressive or amorous, but in each case the details of behavioral expression are related to an individual history which cannot be created by ESB. The classical methods of punishment and reward through normal inputs are more effective in inducing purposeful changes in behavioral activity than the modifications of emotional tuning evoked by cerebral stimulation. Several of the psychoactive drugs may be nearly as effective and are far simpler to use.[21]

c. We must accept the reality that different degrees of behavioral control have been practiced since immemorial times, are widely used at present, and will expand in the future. . . . To discuss whether human behavior can or should be controlled is naïve and misleading. We should discuss what kinds of controls are ethical, considering the efficiency and mechanisms of existing procedures and the desirable degree of these and other controls in the future.[22]

4. *What kinds of possibilities are there for the "far" future?*

a. If you can use computer technology to send an unmanned space satellite to the moon, then it doesn't seem utterly impossible that one day our computers will be sophisticated enough to be used to put thoughts into people's heads. At any rate, one could possibly exert some influence on gross emotional behavior. Suppose, for instance, there were someone with uncontrollable rage reactions which were due to something detectable in the nervous system. The computer could send back a stimulus to inhibit that response. I don't think *that's* science fiction.[23]

b. Sooner or later, someone will decide to put a small computer in the human brain to try and raise intelligence.[24]

c. It would certainly be fascinating to experience some of the memories of a lion or tiger or of one's own pet dog or cat.[25]

d. Figure out a way to make the cells continue to divide just one more time—and, presto, the brain has doubled in size.[26]

e. The vision of a future replete with warehouses full of disembodied brains, all plugged into stimulation tapes or being educated to solve complex scientific, social, or creative problems is not so impossible after all.[27]

QUESTIONS

1. In cases of conviction for crimes resulting from violent or assaultive behavior should a new alternative of electrosurgery (via ESB) be made available in lieu of imprisonment or a death penalty? Should such an option be exercised only by voluntary consent of the convicted or should society have the right to make this decision for the individual?

2. ESB is currently being investigated as a method for treating or curing many maladies such as Parkinson's disease, epilepsy, etc. Should this type of work be extended into the realm of treating or curing psychoses or neuroses, either by the use of programmed stimulation or allowing for control by the individual via self-stimulation?

3. Is there any difference ethically or morally in a "cerebral pacemaker" which can be used to control brain activity and a "heart pacemaker" which can be (and is) used to control heart activity?

4. If a person wanted to have an electrode implanted in his "pleasure" or "sex" center, should he be allowed to do so?

5. Should there be developed professionally staffed centers where interested people could go to stimulate a brain electrode that they had previously had implanted?

6. What about experiments designed to keep a brain

alive after the body dies? Should we attempt to establish communication (electrically or sensory) with such a "living" brain?

7. Suppose researchers found a chemical that could be injected into a yet unborn baby (or a week-old one) that would result in a large increase in the ability of the brain to learn (say, by increasing the number of brain cells or by facilitating the development of interneuron connection and communication in the brain) so that the I.Q. was raised by 50 points, thus making what is today a normal person into a "genius." Should this be a matter of choice for each individual set of parents or should it be done to all children? How would you feel if it was not done to your child when he found himself (or herself) in a first-grade class in which *all or most* of the other kids had much higher I.Q.'s as a result of receiving this treatment?

8. To relieve suffering from a type of epilepsy, it has been found necessary in some cases to completely sever the *corpus callosum* (the bundle of nerves that provides communication between the two sides of the brain). It has been shown that persons with this kind of "split brain" actually have two separate brains which can learn independently. What would we say if such a technique makes possible the development of two separate personalities in the same body? Or for some science fiction: What possibilities might exist if one half of "Moe's" brain were connected to one half of "Charlie's" brain?

9. If researchers are ever successful in hooking together

a brain and a computer so that they communicate with each other by trading knowledge, what would this do to our view of man? of evolution? of God?

10. Is there any difference between the mind and the soul?

6

Sex and the Single Cell

> After thousands of years during which reproduction depended on the union of male and female, man stands ready in the next decade or two to reproduce his own image independently. . . . But we do not yet know what it means to be male or female in this brave new world of ours.[1]

He who dreams no dreams crafts no future. In this chapter we shall consider some of the recent discoveries in the realm of cellular biology. They are the stuff of which the dreams of tomorrow are made. And how we dream determines the future.

The capacity to grow is one of the dramatic characteristics of life that we take for granted. Everything that grows, somewhere at sometime, had its humble beginnings in a single cell. No, single cell sex is nothing new to Mother Nature. Indeed, in the course of aeons of selective probing into the matter of propagation of life, an incredible variety of satisfactory solutions have stood the test of time. Numerous contrasts exist in the web of life; for example, the gestation period for the Asiatic elephant is an average of twenty-one to twenty-two months, but the protozoan glaucoma can reproduce by splitting (binary fission) once every three hours, thus generating 512 descendants in one day. Or to look at it from the point of view of the size of the package used in reproduction, one can contrast the whale-shark's egg of eleven inches in length and five inches in width, which is the largest egg of any living animal, with the seeds of the epiphytic orchids which measure out at something like thirty-five million to the ounce. The speed of attaining reproductive ability also has a wide range of limits as witnessed by the golden hamster female which can reach sexual maturity in twenty-six days, whereas the rare tropical herb *Puya raimondii* has been observed to flower only after some 150 years of life. But no matter what the method of reproduction is, whether asexual or bisexual, fast or slow, it all starts somewhere with a single cell.

It is not the intent of this discussion to show that man is now ready to circumvent Mother Nature by creating some totally new tricks which bypass the single cell beginning. Rather, the point to be made is that man is tinkering with a kind of subterfuge of the selective successes of Mother Nature which finds ways of sexual reproduction that are not the normal mode of operation for a particular species, be it plant or animal. The biologist's knowledge of reproduction has now become so encompassing that it is possible to venture into the realm of *man-selected* manipulation of the fundamental processes. In short, it is an attempt to reconstruct the basic elements into some novel avenues of sexual reproduction. Therefore, the title "Sex and the Single Cell" is meant to focus on the fact that by starting with a single cell, techniques are being discovered whereby man can control the coded information that goes into a beginning cell. In this manner it is possible to "re-create" an exact duplicate of an organism based on information previously coded by ordinary bisexual reproduction. Perhaps someday we will even be able to assemble the coded information in a new way and create entirely novel organisms heretofore unseen in the stream of life.

In order to illustrate the new possibilities, four topics will be discussed: (1) cell nucleus transplantation: clonal reproduction, (2) cell fusion, (3) multiple parenthood or mosaic reproduction, and (4) one-parent cell lines. It is necessary to put in at the beginning the warning that there are often considerable gaps between what are basic principles of cellular biology and what are in fact actually realizable techniques. Nevertheless, this overview of the rapidly moving area of cell biology can provide us with information for an insight into the new fork in the road of knowledge that is presently being mapped out and explored. One thing is already certain, subtle and sophisticated manipulation of the age-old processes of sex is within sight. Asexual reproduction of humans may become a reality along with the familiar bisexual method.

CELL NUCLEUS TRANSPLANTATION: CLONAL REPRODUCTION

Let us begin with an example from the world of plants. Although it does not involve a cell nucleus transplant, it does establish some basic ideas about the process of starting with a single cell in a new way. In the course of investigations of the environmental and cellular requirements necessary for plant reproduction, F. C. Steward achieved the growth of carrot plants in 1962 by a rather unique process. The basic idea is that by appropriate manipulation, single cells were isolated from a carrot root (the part we eat). When they were placed in a special nutrient medium, it was observed that after a time some of the single cells began to grow in an "organized" manner so that after a suitable number of cell divisions a mass of cells was obtained that could be planted in soil to grow into a mature, and in every way normal, adult carrot plant. In other words, it was possible to bypass the normal bisexual reproduction of carrot plants. This type of asexual process means that it would be possible, if we wanted to go to the effort and trouble, to grow literally thousands of *identical* carrot plants—all from the same carrot root! Fundamentally, two basic ideas about cell growth and development were established by this procedure: mature carrot plants can be asexually grown from single cells and all the carrot plants produced must necessarily have the exact genetic makeup of the original "parent" carrot root. In passing, we can mention that subsequent work has shown that this same kind of reproductive process is successful with tobacco plants, aspen trees, asparagus, Queen Anne's lace, and some orchids.

One result of this experimentation has been to force us to review in a new light the classical division of cells into two categories, namely, somatic (body cells incapable of reproduction) and germ (sperm or egg cells capable of reproduction when joined together). In terms of genetic information carrying ability, a somatic cell carries a double set of chromosomes, having received a single set from each parent. Such a cell is called diploid. The germ cells, on the other hand, have only a single set of chromosomes and are called haploid. Bisexual reproduction requires the combination of two appropriate germ cells (the egg and the sperm) to produce a single cell called a zygote. This zygote contains the double set of genetic or chromosomal information that is needed as instructions for a new organism.

Seen in this light, Steward's accomplishment was to take a somatic cell with a diploid number of chromosomes, and by isolating it in a proper environment, it was "fooled" into believing it was a zygote again. This is clear demonstration of the fact that even though a somatic cell of a carrot has differentiated into a root cell (as opposed, say, to a cell in the green top), the genetic information with which to make a whole new carrot plant is still intact. All one has to do is put the cell back into its "original" environment in order to start the developmental process all over again.

Because a genetically uniform mass of cells is known as a clone (from the Greek word meaning "throng"), in popular terminology this process is known as cloning. In fact, the familiar gardening trick of placing a branch or plant cutting in the ground in order to grow a mature plant is a clonal reproduction method—direct descendance from a single individual. The genius of Steward's demonstration lies in that he started with the simplest possible piece of coherent information—a single cell.

The process of transplanting a nucleus from one cell to another represents another approach to clonal reproduction. It is based on a very simple idea: replace the nucleus of an egg cell with a nucleus from a somatic cell from any member of the same species. Then by placing

this new cell in the zygotic environment, growth can occur along normal lines to produce eventually an adult,
mature organism. In other words, the egg cell with its
haploid nucleus cannot do it by itself until in some manner it gets a full set of genetic instructions (in this case
provided by the diploid somatic nucleus).

To move into the animal world we find that in the
early 1950's Drs. Robert W. Briggs and Thomas R. King
demonstrated that it was possible to replace the egg cell
nucleus of a freshly fertilized egg cell of the leopard frog
(*Rana pipiens*) with one taken from a piece of embryonic
tissue. Armed with these diploid instructions, the egg cell
went through a normal development into a tadpole and
eventually an adult leopard frog. In 1961, J. B. Gurdon
and co-workers at Oxford were able to test this idea
further by using a totally differentiated intestinal cell
nucleus (a somatic cell) in place of the not so highly
differentiated embryonic one. They had the same success
—adult frogs grew from nuclear transplanted eggs. A
minor difference was that they used the South African
clawed toad (*Xenopus laevis*). In actual practice the
transplant technique is not overly difficult since the frog
cells and their nuclei are large enough to be manipulated
under microscopic vision with micromanipulating tools
and pipettes.

Again the essential point is that the genetic material
in a somatic cell is not lost or permanently inactivated
even if that cell has differentiated for the specific role of
an intestinal cell in a frog. The diploid nucleus still re-
tains the coded information necessary to go through the
entire process of reproducing another mature individual.
The startling extension of such an idea to a mammal is

that possibly every somatic cell in the adult species, whether it be skin, hair, or intestine, has the potential information available for the creation of a new genetically identical individual. In theory all one has to do is find the proper way to "switch" that information back on by re-creating the zygotic environment and providing for the usual conditions for development. Of course, the hooker for mammals is that the zygotic environment is quite a bit more complex than that of a frog or a carrot plant. For example, all the frog's development occurs outside the body of the female parent from the time of fertilization to the self-feeding tadpole stage. Even though researchers have been able to grow mice and human embryos (produced either by normal or test-tube fertilization) for a period of days in a culture medium, all attempts have failed to "implant" this embryo into the uterine environment for subsequent development. (However, it is quite possible that by the time you read these words, such attempts will have been successful.)

CELL FUSION

Cells with more than one nucleus have been known since the 1830's; however, the controlled laboratory production and manipulation of cells with more than one nucleus was not achieved until 1960, when a team of three researchers, G. Barski, S. Sorieul, and F. Cornefert reported that they had observed fusion between two different lines of mouse cells which were growing together in the same culture medium. They showed that it was possible to produce a new type of cell which contained in one nucleus chromosomal material from two different cells. Five years later another step on the ladder was taken when Harris and Watkins reported using an inactivated Sendai virus to fuse together somatic cells from two different animal species. These hybrid cells (called heterokaryons) were viable, i.e., living. This observation has created a flurry of work in the area of cell fusion as cell biologists hurried to push it to its limits. Three important points have been established by this work: (1) a general method exists for fusing animal cells together; (2) fusion can be induced between cells from widely different species, say, man-mouse, mouse-hamster, man-mosquito, and indeed, almost every conceivable combination between human cells and those of the common laboratory animals, birds, and frogs; and (3) these heterokaryons are capable of continued growth and division.

This may not appear too startling at first since the process of nucleus fusion is the basis of the familiar process of egg and sperm cell union to produce a zygote. However, the staggering idea here is that cell fusion is possible across species boundaries. We ordinarily think of species as referring to a group of animals or plants which breed among themselves to produce fertile offspring having the characteristics of the parents. That is to say, the usual meaning centers on the inability of different species to mix cells sexually. If the technique of cell fusion of somatic or germ cells between species is ever developed as a starting point for producing "offspring," then a new way of generating species will be at hand. Man will have wrested another task from Mother Nature. (Of course, crossing between species does occur, as in the case of the mule being the result of the sexual union of a horse and an ass.)

The exact details of cell fusion are not essential to our discussion (indeed, they are not yet known), however, the general slant of the picture seems to be that the covering of the virus cell (the viral envelope) is in some way responsible for creating an initial bridge between the two cells which leads to complete fusion of cellular material inside one cell wall. Not all heterokaryons (fused cells) are capable of indefinite multiplication. Some of the multinucleate cells (two, three, four, or more nuclei can be present in various combinations between the two species) can remain alive for several weeks; however, continued reproduction depends upon the ability to form daughter cells which contain a single nucleus. Numerous pathways exist for this fusion at the time of cell division (mitosis) so that the heterokaryon gives rise to two mononucleate daughter cells (called synkaryons). Difficulties do not stop here; however, we shall stop our discussion to avoid getting bogged down in technical details.

Where can this knowledge of cell fusion lead us? The answer is a multiple one—in many directions. Four of them can serve as illustrations.

1. The availability of the Harris-Watkins technique for cell fusion has generated a powerful new tool for answering questions about how cells communicate with each other. For example, it has been shown that a hen cell nucleus can understand signals emanating from the cytoplasm (everything in the cell exclusive of the nucleus) of a human or mouse cell. That is, cells of different species can communicate! Even mild speculation on the future implications of this discovery indicate that understanding the rules of the game on the cellular level might

lead to some startling new developments. Who knows what can happen if we start trading information between man and mouse cells? (If cloning and cell fusion are ever combined, as they no doubt will be, the old cliché "Are you a man or a mouse?" will have to take on a new meaning.)

2. Through investigation of cell fusion we will undoubtedly learn more about the way in which genes operate. (Genes are small chemical units located on chromosomes which are responsible for development and transmission of genetic information, i.e., protein synthesis, color of eyes, height, etc.) It turns out that although initially a fused cell often contains one set of chromosomes from each parent cell, continual growth and division occur with a slow but progressive loss of chromosomes. By following this loss, we will eventually be able to "map" the human chromosomes. The implications for genetic engineering are obvious.

3. Evidence is accumulating to support a rather stunning conclusion, namely, that there do not appear to be mechanisms in individual cells for the recognition of incompatibility between species or individuals. This is quite in contrast with the situation in tissue or organ transplants where mechanisms exist for recognizing and eventually rejecting foreign tissue. It is quite possible, then, that additional knowledge on the cellular level will shed light on the rejection processes in tissues which are responsible for the major problem with organ transplants.

4. James D. Watson, of Nobel Prize fame and writer of the best seller *The Double Helix,* had this to say in a 1971 Congressional hearing about what may be an important payoff to come from cell-fusion research.

The cell fusion technique now offers one of the best avenues for understanding the genetic basis of cancer. Today all over the world, cancer cells are being fused with normal cells to pinpoint those specific chromosomes responsible for given forms of cancer. In addition, fusion techniques are the basis of many genetic efforts to unravel the biochemistry of diseases like cystic fibrosis or multiple sclerosis.[2]

MULTIPLE PARENTHOOD
OR MOSAIC REPRODUCTION

Two mothers—two fathers: all for the same mouse. You're putting me on! Multiple parenthood for the same offspring is another offshoot of the concept of cell fusion.

Here is how it's done: Take two pure black mice (at this time preferably of opposite sex) and mate them to get a fertilized egg. Take two pure white mice and do the same. After eight cell divisions in each embryo, remove them from the respective mother's oviduct, place each in a special culture growth medium, add a chemical to dissolve the covering membrane around each embryo, and gently push the two embryos together to form a single aggregate mass. If the combined cell continues to grow, it can be transferred to the prepared uterus of a foster mother mouse for development and eventually birth. The physical appearance of the resulting offspring will be one of the following: pure white, pure black, a patchwork of black and white, or black and white striping!

Hundreds of such mosaic mice have now been produced by Dr. Beatrice Mintz in an effort to unravel the mysteries of cell growth and differentiation as controlled by genetic information. Although the various colorings of the four-parent mice are striking, the internal differences are much more so. In some, the internal organs have two different genetic types of cells in them, and in others a particular organ comes from only one set of parents. In other words, a mouse may have a heart inherited from one set of parents, a liver from the other, and blood from both.

Other possible combinations of parent sets have also been tried with success: short-lived strain with a long-lived strain; health-prone strain with a disease-prone strain; and cancer-prone strain with noncancer-prone strain. All these experimental designs are expected to shed new light on how the developmental evolution of a cell population is tied to genetic mechanisms.

One-Parent Cell Lines

Can a single egg cell be persuaded to grow and divide without the cooperation of its natural partner, a sperm cell? And how about the reverse, sperm cell growth without an egg? The answer to both questions is now yes. In terms of information carrying capacity, the problem boils down to the following. As we saw earlier, egg and sperm cells are haploid—that is, they contain only half the normal number of chromosomes necessary to direct the development to an adult organism. If a haploid cell line could be established, this "half information" situation would provide a powerful tool for the geneticist in that it would allow for simple and direct experiments on mutations in individual chromosomes.

In 1970, Jerome Freed and Liselotte Mezger-Freed achieved success in obtaining a haploid cell line by some elegant manipulation of fertilized eggs of the frog *Rana pipiens*. The technique used was to remove the maternal nucleus from a fertilized egg before it had a chance to fuse with the sperm nucleus. Then with some luck and the proper environment, development of the cell proceeds under directions from the cytoplasm of the egg and the nucleus of the sperm. This simple description far understates the considerable technical difficulty in achieving this success. It came only when one frog was found with a genetic makeup somehow suitable for yielding a stable line of haploid cells grown for over 150 successive generations in culture.

Reader's with backgrounds in biology will have realized at the outset of this section that we are talking about the process of parthenogenesis, or reproduction by the development of an unfertilized egg, or even more simply—virgin birth. Naturally occurring parthenogenesis is not an unusual thing in nature as it is found in certain insects, crustaceans, and worms. Experimental virgin birth goes back into the late 1800's when it was discovered that something as simple as a pinprick on an egg of a sea anemone would induce monosexual development. Success has also been achieved with frogs and rabbits and at least as far as the initial stages of development in the mouse. Typically, though, parthenogenesis is the female-oriented concept in that the start is made from an egg cell. The work of Freed, however, shows that it is possible to establish a cell line from the male counterpart, the sperm.

As often happens in science, a breakthrough on one front, in this case the haploid frog cell cultures, is quickly followed by other related advances. Three such situations arose in rapid succession after the publication of Freed's work. A Polish group at the University of Warsaw (Andrzcy Tarkowski and others) were able to trigger mouse eggs to grow and divide by the procedure of electric shock while the eggs were still in the oviduct. Some of the shock-activated eggs developed into "fatherless" embryos. When attempts were made to implant them in the uterus of a female mouse, the implantation was successful for only a short period of time and none of the embryos survived to full term. Christopher Graham, at Oxford, has taken a chemical approach to the problem of activating parthenogenesis, the major result of which has been a culture of haploid cells that survived several months. In both of these mouse experiments, some of the cells in study spontaneously doubled their chromosome number to become diploid, thus generating in effect one-parent cells with the normal amount of chromosomal information. Graham succeeded in bringing some to full term, but the exact mechanism, significance, and relationship to the mother have not yet been reported.

The third example concerns work done by Norman Sunderland with tobacco plants. Here it has been possible to obtain adult haploid tobacco plants by growth started from a tobacco anther (male germ cell) placed in a suitable nutrient medium. Since it has been found that some of the growing haploid cells spontaneously double their chromosomes to become diploid, the possibility of producing diploid plants from a single parent is being actively pursued. Such a technique would no doubt be another step in a long series of developments that have drastically revolutionized the agricultural world in the past century.

SUMMARY

Normal bisexual development proceeds from the initial fertilization of an egg to the subsequent division of the zygote into two, four, eight, sixteen, thirty-two, and eventually millions upon millions of cells, the collection of which is a man or a mouse. And even though those millions upon millions of cells are divided into organs (heart, liver, etc.), nerves, blood, bone, and muscles, each and every cell carries the original set of information fused together in the union of two germ nuclei. This in brief outline is Mother Nature's selective solution to the continued propagation of men and mice. Nothing in modern cell biology has changed these facts. They are given, if a mature organism is to be produced. Someday enough knowledge might be in hand to conceive of a different solution to the problem of reproduction, but that is far into the future. The current threshold of knowledge is awesome enough. It says: look, we can control what information gets into that initial cell—by cell nucleus transplantation, nucleus fusion, or parthenogenetic activation. Therefore, we can control what eventually comes out of that cell. That, friends, is what the new rule book of sex says. Same game; same players; new set of rules.

7

The Birds and Bees Revisited

For there is hope for a tree,
    if it be cut down, that it will sprout
    again,
and that its shoots will not cease. . . .
If a man die, shall he live again?
                              (Job 14:7, 14a.)

Unless something happens to change the direction of flow of knowledge from the area of reproductive biology, the people who write "birds and bees" books for children are going to have to add some new chapters and be prepared to revise them often. After many millennia utilizing the kind of bisexual reproduction selected for man, we now find ourselves having to confront the possibility of some drastic changes—some new options for old methods. As we are well aware, one of the crises that has spilled over into the 1970's is the environmental concern; however, without doing more than mentioning it, I would like to extract out of that concern one irrevocable fact: we have literally blundered blindly into our present predicament and have begun to do something about it *only after* we have considerably fouled the very nest we live in. In a nutshell, we have run out of corners to put our "junk" into, whether it be raw sewage, beer cans, or auto exhaust.

So what, then, is the connection between pollution and sex? I once heard an eminent scientist in a public address argue that even if it were possible, no one in his right mind would want to use clonal reproduction methods on humans. Animals, no doubt; but humans, definitely not. But naïve as I might be that *is* precisely the point. Think again about how badly and knowingly we fumbled the environment problem. Now wonder a bit as to the consequences of a fumble in the area of reproduction in the chance that someday researchers might decide to do the improbable and apply these techniques to humans. To me there is just no doubt; changes in the way in which the human race is sexually propagated will have a profound impact on the meaning of individual identity and the meaning of existence. I do not mean by this that this is necessarily good or bad. A person only has to contemplate his own reaction to someday meeting "himself"—a "self" that had been cloned from one of his cells. Shaking hands with "yourself" would surely be a profound experience, perhaps ecstatic for some and shattering for others. In other words, there are on our foreseeable horizon some situations in which the stakes involved are not only the values emanating from our sexual past, which have been based on the dual path stemming from the age-old tradition of boy-meets-girl, but also the very meaning of manhood or womanhood—this is, assuming male and female identity remain important for reproduction.

The point to consider is that we have not yet used

these methods of reproduction, and so theoretically we have a chance to talk about them before we do. I am not going to argue that we should not use this knowledge because we don't know what the impact or results will be. I am trying to say that we should begin to develop ways of paying attention to implications and value spin-offs from the use of science, before and during, not just after we do something (and here our record is miserably poor: witness the environmental scene). It is no argument not to do something because we don't know what will happen. Nevertheless, I think it is possible to understand better the meaning of "humanness" on this poverty- and color-torn planet, so that if we do clone humans, for example, we will know why and for what purpose we do it and not just because it was there to be done.

Again we should point out that the extension of clonal reproduction from carrot plants and frogs to mammals such as mice and men is certainly a large jump in complexity. Nevertheless no one seems to doubt that given the time and effort the extension will be made. And when it is made there will be some rather incredible options on our doorstep. Try these four for openers: (1) see "yourself" born nine months after implanting a cloned cell with your nucleus in a host pregnant woman, (2) auto-adultery in which a woman gives birth to "herself" via a cloned cell with one of her nuclei, (3) a kind of serial immortality by having yourself cloned before or after you "die" (Henry Jones III may take on a completely new meaning), and (4) multiple copies (5, 10, 20, or 100) of a single individual (shades of the Bokanovsky process from Huxley's *Brave New World*). Immediately a swarm of questions gets released. Who decides who gets cloned? How will clones feel about themselves? How will unclones feel about clones? Will clones be allowed to marry unclones, or only clones, or nobody? Are clones legal heirs? Which is better—one hundred Einsteins, one hundred Raquel Welchs, or one hundred Charlie Browns? Will a group of identical clones be able to communicate with each other in a way better than unclones, say by some type of ESP? Etc. and etc.

Before we go farther perhaps two things should be mentioned. First, natural clones already exist in the persons of identical twins, and second, although clones would be genetically identical, each one would have a unique and different set of experiences while growing up and thus would be a "different" individual. Another Einstein would not necessarily discover relativity; he might take a different fork in the road the "second time" around and stick to his post as a patent clerk.

In regard to the other reproductive methods mentioned earlier, we can also do the same kind of speculative thinking. What would we think of a person who had only one parent? Four? Ten? Remember the old jokes about what would happen if one animal was crossed with another? (Example: a mink crossed with a kangaroo gives a mink coat with pockets. Help! I need a better example.) If cell-fusion experiments result in totally new species, then they will no doubt make the rounds again.

But rather than pursue this line of speculative thinking farther, let us turn our attention to the kinds of challenges that exist in regard to the meaning of that catch-all word "sex." To begin with, it seems clear that we are traveling in the direction of being able to separate the act of intercourse from that of procreation or reproduction. Modern techniques have already provided new options for intercourse without procreation in "the pill" and the IUD (intrauterine device) and for the opposite situation of procreation without intercourse (artificial insemination—now some ten to twenty thousand births a year in the United States). Even though these techniques have come about only in the past few generations, it is already evident that they are playing a role in our changing attitudes toward sex. Just since the early 1900's we have changed from treating sex as a taboo subject even between friends to its acceptance in casual conversation between strangers. Or stated in another way, we have seen a change from Victorian guilt if one did experience sex to a Kinseyian guilt if one didn't experience sex. The rapidity with which we have moved from Freud (an awareness of sex in terms of psychological problems) to Kinsey (a statistical awareness of sex, i.e., the number of times becomes important) to Masters and Johnson (a technique awareness, i.e., how it is done becomes important) is really an incredible change. And in fact, it leads me to wonder whether or not our modern focus on orgasm as the ultimate experience (particularly in a simultaneous sense) has not already in a subtle fashion prepared us for the appearance of the actual techniques of reproduction that occur without intercourse. That is to say, is it possible that we are already moving psychologically into a new awareness of sex so that in reality the acceptance of alternate methods of reproduction will not be earthshaking and society-rending when they finally do arrive?

Certainly it is too early to tell where we will come out, but it seems to me indisputable that we are in a period of redefinition of the meaning of the act of intercourse or to put it in broader terms, the meaning of the use of the body. Although not many realized it at the time, the introduction of "the pill" was the final event in a series of contraceptive methods (rhythm method, cheap condoms, foams and douches) that removed the fear of pregnancy from the sexual act and thereby opened up the whole area for redefinition.

The meaning and role of male/female and father/ mother is also being redefined. There is not space to go into the Women's Liberation Movement in a book like this, but surely this is a serious effort that will inevitably change our concepts of "man" and "woman." The movement has many dimensions; however, an important one does center around the role and place of maternal functions. As more and more women begin to express themselves in fuller human terms and to create a new level of sexual equality, we can wonder what will happen to the traditional notion that a woman's role is to serve as the carrier, deliverer, and raiser of children. It is much too early to guess what impact the new options for reproduction will have on what it means to be a woman. The only thing we can guess for sure is that how we choose to use this new knowledge will have a direct and profound impact.

In my view, the place where these two major points meet—the act of intercourse and the meaning of manhood and womanhood—is precisely at the point of expression of individuality: the meaning of "I" or "me." The significant thing to note is that this cannot be fully understood except in terms of other persons, i.e., individuality is defined in terms of relationship. Rollo May, in his book *Love and Will,* treats this subject in great length. Perhaps the following two statements will capture the essence of his discussion:

> For human beings, the more powerful need is not for sex per se but for relationship, intimacy, acceptance, and affirmation.[1]
> The paradox of love is that it is the highest degree of awarness of the self as a person and the highest degree of absorption in the other.[2]

May goes on to speak of the personal nature of the love act in a way that illustrates that the expression of individuality and of relationship reaches a significant peak in that experience.

> The fact that love is personal is shown in the love act itself. Man is the only creature who makes love *face to face,* who copulates looking at his partner.[3]

Granted there are variations on the classical face-to-face position, but this posture does the following:

> This opens the whole front of the person—the breasts, the chest, the stomach, all the parts which are most tender and most vulnerable—to the kindness or the cruelty of the partner.[4]

And in so doing, both partners are at the same time aware of each other's response—whether of ecstasy, indifference or pain, and in May's words: "It is the posture of the ultimate baring of one's self." [5] How we shall relate the dual-personalness of the love act and the experience of "baring of one's self" to the act of procreation is the question of our future.

In the opening pages of *Brave New World,* the Director of the Central London Hatchery and Conditioning Center refers to the words "mother" and "father" which are in that day considered smut. " 'These,' he says gravely, 'are the unpleasant facts; I know it. But then most historical facts *are* unpleasant.' " [6] I am not convinced that the words "mother" and "father" are going to become the unpleasant facts of our future, even though I am convinced that the facts of reproduction are going to change. Whatever we do with regard to making use of them for human procreation, I hope that it will be done with a view toward "relationship, intimacy, acceptance, and affirmation." These are human realities that surely will change in meaning, but as long as they are central to what we do as individuals and in-relationship, they will not become unpleasant historical facts. If they do, man and woman are undone.

REASONS
TO FAVOR OR OPPOSE

For purposes of organizing discussion the listing of reasons is divided into three categories: (1) clonal reproduction, (2) single or higher than two parenthood, and (3) cell fusion followed by clonal reproduction. Overlap between these areas is to be expected, so where it seems to you appropriate in terms of adding strength to an argument one way or another, do not hesitate to cross the lines of these categories.

In order to avoid unnecessary repetition, it is assumed that each of the following positions applies to any of the new methods of reproduction.

1. We should do it, if we can do it, on the grounds that new knowledge gained often leads to positive advances that are unpredictable until the effort is made. The converse is possible also, in that the new knowledge gained might lead to advances termed negative (for example, production of a sterile race incapable of further reproduction, and thus extinction as a species).

2. Just because we can do it is not a valid reason for doing it. There are some things that should be left undone.

3. It's just not "natural," therefore we shouldn't do it. Man should not tamper with the workings of nature.

CLONAL REPRODUCTION

Reasons to Favor

1. Direct copying of a superior person (i.e., genotype); would not have to construct one by lengthy process of genetic engineering over a period of many generations.

2. Genetic immortality of superior genotypes; also perhaps a new twist in the age-old concept of immortality in that a "person" could live successive lives (although not having experiential contact with those previous lives).

3. To control selection of sex of offspring (and thereby avoiding the passage of sex-linked inferior genes).

4. To provide a supply of interchangeable parts for transplantation; would avoid rejection problems if

the transplanted material was of the same genetic makeup.

5. To investigate modes of communication between genetically identical persons; this situation does occur naturally with multiple births resulting from cleavage of the fertilized egg (i.e., identical twins)—the advantage here would lie in the possibility of large numbers of genetically identical persons.

6. To investigate the role of environmental influences by "raising" a number of identical clones in completely different environments and cultures.

7. To discover whether, in a new cultural environment and time in history, a cloned copy of a genius would outdo the "original."

Reasons to Oppose

1. Bypasses the mixing of genes through random mating and sexual reproduction; this type of diversity has been the strength of natural selection, i.e., by continually creating new combinations of genes and then subsequent selection of those which are most favorable for survival.

2. Possibility of production of grossly malformed or malfunctioning humans as a result of a malfunction or imperfection in the nucleus chosen for transplantation (not all frogs that are cloned are normal).

3. A violation of the natural method of sexual reproduction in terms of an assault on the nature of human parenthood.

4. Reproductively speaking, could result in a dead-end street for two reasons: (a) clones could be sterile (a somewhat higher proportion of cloned frogs are sterile than would be found in a normal population) and (b) if clones were to begin reproducing, say, after a few clonal-generations of compulsory sterilization, they would be dumping a load of harmful genes into the gene pool.

5. Possibility of a new type of "self-identity" crisis when the clonite is old enough to reflect on his origin.

SINGLE OR HIGHER THAN TWO PARENTHOOD

Reasons to Favor

1. Scientific curiosity; similar experimental methods have provided us with new knowledge leading to stronger and better hybrid strains of plants and animals.

2. Would provide a totally new avenue for mixing of genes; might introduce a new vigor into the human species.

3. Might make it possible to breed into a person resistance to disease or aging or to greatly increase intelligence by blending in genes from other parents.

4. Possible advantages for organ transplantation; if have genetic input from more than two parents, it might increase the chances of matching up with tissue of a donor organ.

Reasons to Oppose

1. Possibility of enhanced expression of harmful genes, either by pairing of genes from one parent or from a combination of, say, four parents.

2. Perhaps organ transplants would become more difficult because of some newly developed type of rejection.

3. Same reasons as for opposition to cloning; in particular, possibility of grossly malformed or malfunctioning humans (#2) and a violation of the nature of human parenthood (#3).

CELL FUSION FOLLOWED BY CLONAL REPRODUCTION

Reasons to Favor

1. Creation of new and novel species.

2. Addition of humanoid intelligence into primates or other animals so they could be used for routine work (such as earth or ocean mining, assembly-line production, or various types of data collection).

Reasons to Oppose

1. Possibility of grossly malformed or malfunctioning "subhumans."

2. Same objections as in clonal reproduction.

VIEWS FOR REFLECTION

1. *What are some of the ethical, value, and cultural factors involved in new methods of reproduction which bypass the traditional way?*

a. We need to raise the ethical questions with a serious and not a frivolous conscience. A man of frivolous conscience announces that there are ethical quandaries ahead that we must urgently consider before the future catches up with us. By this he often means that we need to devise a new ethics that will provide the rationalization for doing in the future what men are bound to do because of new actions and interventions science will have made possible. In contrast, a man of serious conscience means to say in raising urgent ethical questions that there may be some things that men should never do.[7]

b. Four questions, crucial in making a proper response to the issues raised by the new biology: (1) the question of whether or not man has or can reasonably be expected to have the wisdom to become his own creator, the unlimited lord of the future; (2) the anthropological and basic ethical question concerning the nature and meaning of human parenthood, and of actions that would be destructive of parenthood as a basic form of humanity; (3) the questionableness of actions and interventions that are consciously set within the context of aspirations to godhood; and (4) the question of human species-suicide.[8]

c. There is no urgent social problem to be addressed by such a technique. It does serve as a metaphor to indicate that future generations will have infinitely more powerful ways than we do to deal with whatever they may regard as socially urgent issues of human nature. We can therefore focus more confidently on dealing with the distress of individual human beings in the immediate generation. . . . Cloning-a-man is one of the least important questions I can think of; "who must be held accountable for the next generation and how" may be the most important question.[9]

d. And in the literary, social, and political areas the cultural climate surely plays so large a role that there may be little basis for expecting outstanding achievement to be continued by a scion. The world might thus be quite disappointed by the contributions of another Tolstoy, Churchill, or Martin Luther King, or even another Newton or Mozart. Moreover, though experience with monozygotic twins is somewhat reassuring, persons produced by copying might suffer from a novel kind of "identity crisis." Though our system of values clearly places us under moral obligation to do everything possible to cure disease, there is no comparable basis for using cloning to advance culture.[10]

2. *What impact would clonal reproduction have on the notion of parenthood?*

a. We procreate new beings like ourselves in the midst of our love for one another, and in this there is a trace of the original mystery by which God created the world because of His love.[11]

b. The "experiment" involved in the thought, Shall we clone a man?, and the technical possibility of doing so on a vast scale, may provide the truly propitious opportunity for acquiring the knowledge that the link between sexual love and procreation is not in us a matter of specific or animal consequence only, but is of truly human and personal import. To put radically asunder what nature and nature's God joined together in parenthood when he made love procreative, to disregard the foundation of the covenant of marriage and the covenant of parenthood in the reality that makes for a least minimally loving procreation, to attempt to soar so high above an eminently human parenthood, is inevitably to fall far below—into a vast technological alienation of man. Limitless dominion over procreation means the boundless servility of man-womanhood.[12]

c. Among the trends imminent for the individual sexual person, it seems most obvious from what we have already said that in human society sexual intercourse is increasingly moving out of the reproductive sphere. Reproduction can and is being achieved with increasing frequency without the benefit of sexual intercourse. Both these trends are clearly contained in the fact that human reproduction is rapidly becoming more and more a matter of deliberate choice on the part of parents. But this also implies that sexual intercourse must now be more fully integrated into our lives with *some meaning other than the mere reproductive*.[13]

d. Finally, the Christian mind, insofar as it takes the Scriptures seriously, is earnest in its understanding of human reproduction as a part of a larger spiritual package. That is to say, the Christian understanding of things views the production of children by an act of sexual love as a sacred thing. Whether it should become a matter of general laboratory procedure, totally cool and objective and devoid of the deeper overtones of the mutual sharing of two devoted and loving persons, is open to serious question. The Christian mind sees a sharp qualitative difference between the desire of two loving persons to reproduce their image in a person who is part of both of them, and the determination to impose one's genotype intact upon carbon copies of himself. The latter seems to the thoughtful Christian to be narcissistic.[14]

3. *What about mishaps?* (*And is this any different from our present situation of naturally occurring deformed children?*)

a. In the case of cloning a man, the question is what to do with mishaps, whether discovered in the course of extracorporeal gestation in the laboratory or by monitored uterine gestation. In case a monstrosity—a subhuman or parahuman individual—results, shall the experiment simply be stopped and this artfully created human life killed? In mingling individual human chromosomes with those of the "higher" mammals (given sufficient dosage and "a few years"), what shall be done if the resulting individual lives seem remarkably human?[15]

b. Paradoxically, the issue of "subhuman" hybrids may arise first, just because of the touchiness of experimentation on obviously human material. Tissue and organ cultures and transplants are already in wide experimental or therapeutic use, but there would be widespread inhibitions about risky experiments leading to an object that could be labelled as a human or parahuman infant. However, there is enormous scientific interest in organisms whose karyotype is augmented by fragments of the human chromosome set, especially as we know so little in detail of man's biological and genetic homology with other primates. (Note: karyotype refers to the type of material in the nucleus of a cell.) [16]

4. *Would it be wise to make partial use of new reproduction techniques where specific goals might be in mind?*

a. "Tempered clonality" would be an attempt to have the best of both worlds: asexual reproduction for uniformity, for intimate communication, and for multiplying proven excellence; sexual reproduction for heterogeneity and innovation. "A mix of sexual and clonal reproduction makes good sense for genetic design. . . . When a suitable type is ascertained take care to maintain it by clonal propagation." [17]

b. Another type of cloning can already be accomplished in mammals: when the relatively undifferentiated cells of an early mouse embryo are gently separated each can be used to start a new embryo. A large set of identical twins can thus be produced. However, they would be copies of an embryo of undetermined genetic structure, rather than of an already known adult. This procedure therefore does not seem tempting in man, unless the production of identical twins (or of greater multiplets) should develop special social values, such as those suggested by Aldous Huxley in *Brave New World*.[18]

c. The possibilities are even more interesting if we should be able to combine both cloning and embryonic fusion. . . . Individual cells from Barbra Streisand could be fused with cells from a leading Music Hall Rockette and a real superstar would be born or decanted. Similar creative combinations might be advantageous in athletics and other fields.[19]

5. *Is it inevitable that these new reproductive techniques will be attempted on humans?*

a. No reason, of course, dictates that such cloning experiments need occur. Most of the medical people capable of such experimentation would probably steer clear of any step which looked as though its real purpose were to clone. But it would be shortsighted to assume that everyone would instinctively recoil from such purposes. Some people may sincerely believe the world desperately needs many copies of really exceptional people if we are to fight our way out of the ever-increasing computer-mediated complexity that makes our individual brains so frequently inadequate.[20]

b. Nor should anyone be frightened out of his ethical wits by grand eugenic designs. It may take some temerity to oppose these grand interferences for man's self-reconstruction and control over the evolutionary future, but this is a not unreasonable position. In the present age the attempt will be made to deprive us of our wits by comparing objections of schemes of progressive genetic engineering or cloning men to earlier opposition to inoculations, blood transfusions, or the control of malaria. These things are by no means to be compared: the practice of medicine in the service of life is one thing; man's unlimited self-modification of the genetic conditions of life would be quite another matter.[21]

c. The belief that surrogate mothers and clonal babies are inevitable because science always moves forward, an attitude expressed to me recently by a scientific colleague, represents a form of laissez-faire nonsense dismally reminiscent of the creed that American business, if left to itself, will solve everybody's problems. Just as the success of a corporate body in making money need not set the human condition ahead, neither does every scientific advance automatically make our lives more "meaningful." No doubt the person whose experimental skill will eventually bring forth a clonal baby will be given wide notoriety. But the child who grows up knowing that the world wants another Picasso may view his creator in a different light.[22]

d. Instead of a nuclear arms race, future generations may find themselves involved in a cloning race to produce ever more brilliant teams of scientists, more courageous soldiers, or more docile public servants.[23]

QUESTIONS

1. Assume that the wife of a childless couple has a blockage in her Fallopian tubes that cannot be corrected by surgery and that prevents her ova from reaching a position to be fertilized by her husband's sperm. If requested, should we permit surgical removal of one of her ova, fertilization in a test tube with her husband's sperm, and then implantation of

the fertilized egg in her womb for subsequent development and birth? What if her husband was sterile? Should a "donor's" sperm be used, if they both agree?

2. Assume that the wife of a childless couple is physically unable to carry a pregnancy to a successful conclusion. Should it be permissible to remove surgically one of her eggs, test-tube fertilize it with her husband's sperm, and then implant the embryo in the womb of an anonymous host mother who would carry it to birth, at which time the newborn child would be "adopted" by the biological parents?

3. Should the same options as in 1 and 2 above be offered to an unmarried woman?

4. If a childless couple wants to adopt a baby, should they someday be given the option of having one cloned for them according to their specifications?

5. In terms of our traditional views of sex, what has been the impact of intercourse without pregnancy (made possible with "the pill" and the IUD) and of pregnancy without intercourse (made possible with artificial insemination)? What additional impact would there be if clonal reproduction or "womb nursing" (i.e., carrying a baby for another woman) became realities?

6. Should embryonic clones of people be kept in cold storage so that in the event of the failure of an organ, a replacement could be grown to take its place?

7. Should we clone a small group of identical individuals and then allow them to grow up in diver-

sified environments in order to get information on the contribution made by the environment to the development of personality, creativity, and intelligence?

8. Should we clone a group of fifty identical persons to go to the moon for the purpose of establishing a colony there? How about a clonal colony on the bottom of the ocean?

9. Suppose a three-year-old child was hit and killed by an automobile. What should be done if the parents requested that a clone of that child be produced in order to "replace" him?

10. In a literal sense, some parents already attempt to "reproduce" themselves in their children. In some cases if they do not turn out a carbon copy (thinking and acting like they do), they feel that their own lives have failed. Would cloning not increase the domineering impulse in some parents to make their children in their own image? What about the family implications of cloning? Are they any different from the presently accepted methods of adoption?

11. Suppose American scientists decided that they would not attempt to clone a human. What should be done, if anything, if scientists in another country decided to try it?

12. If attempts at cloning a human were to be sanctioned, what controls and guidelines should be laid down? By whom? What should happen if a researcher violated these guidelines?

13. If a human is cloned, should there be special legal "rights" or "limits"? (Say, in terms of inheritance, marriage, reproduction, etc.)

14. What reasons are there for and against attempting to clone a person with the caliber of the mind of an Einstein or a Mozart?

15. Should "solitary parenthood" be attempted, i.e., parthenogenetic reproduction?

16. Should "mosaic" reproduction be attempted, i.e., multiple parenthood using genetic material from more than two parents?

17. Should we attempt to create new and novel species by fusing cells from two different species and then transplanting the newly created nucleus to an appropriate egg for subsequent development into a "mature organism"? Should human cells and genetic material be used in this kind of experimentation? human eggs?

18. At the present time doctors and surgeons are licensed to practice on the basis of their demonstrated competency, not only in skillful terms, but also in terms of dedication toward saving life as guided by the Hippocratic Oath. Should a licensing agency be set up for researchers who are attempting to "improve" humans or create new levels of possibility for the human species?

19. The need to control population is a topic of great debate at the moment. Could cloning be a part of the solution to this problem in that it would provide a

ENJOY AND PONDER

Hi and Lois

method of control over the number of children to be "born"?

20. An individual who is produced by cloning would obviously not have an opportunity to give consent to the procedure. Does this present any peculiar ethical responsibilities that are any different from those of normal reproduction?

8

A New World
in the Morning

> . . . the water continually flowed and flowed
> and yet it was always there;
> it was always the same and yet every
> moment it was new.[1]

Life is like a river—flowing into a future that always holds new possibilities. But present-day man in all his arrogance is pitting the knowledge gained in his miniscule life-span against the incomprehensible span of three billion years of evolutionary flow which has brought life and man to this moment. Viewed in this light we are perhaps justified in asking: Why should we really expect any drastic and quick changes in it all? Tomorrow will be like yesterday. What do we mean—"a new world in the morning"?

The answer is simple to state but profound in its implication. Man is standing on a pyramid of knowledge so great that he can now seriously begin to raise the kinds of questions that have the potential of calling forth a New Man. Man will give birth to a New Man. *Homo creatus* will follow Homo sapiens. Powerful mood drugs, electrical stimulation of the brain, and new methods of reproduction are only a few selections from the tip of the iceberg of opportunity that is being uncovered. All the answers are not here now, but on the other hand, in view of what has happened in the past three centuries who can doubt that once science knows how to ask a question, it eventually finds a way to answer it.

In short, I just don't see how we can stop the flow of the river of knowledge. Man is endowed with an insatiable curiosity to know, and I am not aware of anything in his past that suggests that someday he will pull his boat to the shore and say, "I know enough—now I have rebuilt the Garden of Eden because I have subdued the earth." No, it just doesn't work that way. Every good question that gets answered raises in its place dozens of new ones. Newton's famous remark is still as true today as it was three hundred years ago.

> I do not know how I may appear to the world; but to myself I seem to have been only like a boy, playing on the seashore, and diverting myself in now and then finding a smoother pebble or a prettier shell than ordinary, while the great ocean of truth lay all undiscovered before me.[2]

The far-thinking mind of biophysicist John Platt has expressed this human striving in a similarly poetic fashion.

> To be warm and full and free, these are our first needs, . . . but . . . what dissolves and remolds societies unawares is that we also want, like children, to have sweet smells, music, pictures, entertainment, bright lights, and powerful servants. We want to make magic, to run like the wind and to

fly like the birds and talk across miles and be as beautiful as gods and know how everything works.[3]

But now, as we have seen, "to know how everything works" is being applied with new vigor and success to life in general and man in particular. We are embarking on the road toward experimentation with ourselves and are asking the question: *What would we like to be tomorrow?* The new dimension is that this will be a conscious and planned alteration rather than the result of the haphazard fickle finger of fate of the past. We had no qualms when we "subdued" the animal and plant worlds. We have developed chemicals to kill the insects we don't want and created new plants to replace those we don't want. The frontier question of today is: Will man lose his nerve as he faces the prospects of experimenting with himself? Clearly, this is a new kind of ball game, and there are many who will cry out in honest agony that we should not tamper further with man. Save lives, yes; but change the structure of the living nature of man, no. But is there really any doubt that having come this far we shall continue to go on? This does not mean that we must yield to all of the knowledge that comes in the future. There is nothing implicit in knowledge that says that it must be used. It gets used only if someone decides to use it. And that is really the central concern—the use of knowledge.

Some readers may by now be impatient with what they feel to be a mixture of scientific arrogance and idealism. I would defend myself by saying that I am not arguing that man will reach a new kind of effortless, euphoric utopia. Nor will he reach the level of God, the original Creator. Man will remain man. Problems, suffering, and inhumanity to fellowman are not about to be wiped away by the rush of scientific knowledge. Nevertheless I do feel we must deal with the fact that man has a great deal of potential still not developed. In some ways man is like the ocean that beats on the shoreline. It is forever moving and creating new patterns of waves. It is permanent yet always changing, sometimes gentle, sometimes ferocious. The pulsating waves have the potential for creating new patterns of beauty in the sand, as well as for destruction through the fury of a storm. So it is with scientific knowledge. Through it man has gained a powerful measure of control. What he creates or destroys depends in a large measure on himself. He cannot violate the laws of nature, but he can bend them to his will. But even this does not make him God or create an instant utopia.

Nevertheless, I do not mean to imply that the spiritual or religious side of man is unimportant or irrelevant. It is a rather sweeping statement, but in my view the institutional church has created a lot of mythical rationalizations which have led us away from knowing what it means to confront and know the reality of Jesus Christ. The result of church organization has been to box him up into a tidy, clean package that can be placed in an obscure corner of our minds and life. For the most part we are immune to his power to convict us for our inhumanity to fellowman, whether it be the Indochina war, drug abuse, racism, or the rat-infested ghettos. Therefore, it is my hope that the power we are gaining for man to remake man will be coupled with and guided by a new confrontation with the life and power of Jesus Christ. We need a recombination of the spirit of man and the spirit of Jesus. Without this, man's inhumanity to man will doubtless increase. There are many other religious and spiritual viewpoints that can be brought to bear on this problem, and it is not claimed that my persuasion is the ONLY way. Dialogue and contact between these viewpoints is greatly needed.

I do not claim to possess special insight into where we are going or how man will remake man. However, in the rest of this chapter I will chart a path showing the framework of response that I think is our challenge. Filling in this framework with action will be the subject and content of our lives as we move into the future. To do this we will look briefly at four points: (1) wisdom, (2) choice, (3) new consciousness, and (4) man-in-relation.

WISDOM

What we are tomorrow will be a product of the wisdom we use today. In my view the relationship between knowledge and wisdom is a simple one. Knowledge is created by the framework of organization that our minds synthesize as a way of correlating and pulling together the numerous separate pieces of data, experience, or information that come our way. The success or acceptance of different knowledge frameworks is determined, not only by its comprehensiveness (i.e., ability to relate a large amount of information), but also by its predictive success for future experience. A good knowledge framework also helps to ask new questions which lead to new answers which lead, in turn, to an expanded or altered knowledge framework.

However, when we turn to the use of the knowledge, we

enter into the realm of wisdom. In order to apply knowledge there has to be an interaction with some system or experience. Knowledge is used either to change things by its application or not to change them by refusing to apply it. Knowledge, standing alone, is neutral; it is amoral. Knowledge, applied, takes sides; it is moral. And herein lies the central dilemma of the problem. Science has been incredibly successful at producing knowledge. Technology has taken the knowledge frameworks of basic science and applied them to create new goods or services for use by society. We are in our present eco-crisis precisely because neither science (with its pursuit of knowledge) nor society (with its desire for and the use of applied knowledge) has significantly concerned itself with the problem of wisdom. The scientific-technological complex has operated on the basis of the technological imperative (discussed in the first chapter): If you can do it, do it. If society wants (or can be made to think it wants) pesticides, H-bombs, hair spray, nonreturnable bottles, or fancy detergents, then do it. Never mind the problem of the *wisdom* of doing it; that will take care of itself. But let's stop kidding ourselves, we know we shall have to pay the piper someday.

Man is now facing himself as an experimental object. Will he "do it" because it can be done, or will he pause long enough to ask the question of wisdom—Why do it? One of the commonest ways that scientists have attempted to get off the hook has been to say: "Oh, all I do is discover the knowledge. What is done with it is society's problem. Let the politicians decide what to do." Right and wrong. Right, in the sense that the pursuit of knowledge is a concerted effort directed only at discovering knowledge. Outside of the value decision made that this is a worthwhile thing to do, the process is a neutral one in terms of morality. But wrong, in the sense that it is time for scientists to recognize that they can no longer play ostrich with their heads in the lab. They, too, have to ask the question of what can this be used for and why. The use of knowledge is not simply a political problem for someone else. Because science is the initiating agent in the sense of discovering this knowledge, it cannot beg off responsibility for its application and use. In other words, society should ask science: Why are you doing what you are doing? And science should answer.

Let me illustrate with a recent example that concerns a Harvard geneticist, James Shapiro, who was one of a team that announced the first isolation of a pure gene from a strain of bacterial virus (November, 1969). It is clearly recognizable that this work is one of the key steps toward possible genetic manipulation in humans. Shapiro had this to say at the time of the momentous announcement:

> We did this work for scientific reasons, also because it was interesting to do. But scientists generally have the tendency not to think too much about the consequences of their work while doing it. But now that we have, we are not happy about it. This is a problem in all scientific research, the bad consequences we cannot control.[4]

Shortly after this announcement, Shapiro quit science, giving the following reasons: (1) the work he was doing could be put to use for evil purposes by those who control science (government and large corporations) in the same manner as atomic energy was used, (2) his refusal to continue to contribute to a system in which the general public does not have a voice in what science is to be done, and (3) political solutions, not scientific, are urgently needed in the areas of health care and pollution. The point is not to argue Shapiro's reasons for giving up science, but rather to suggest that his original naïveté at not ever stopping to think about the implications of what he was doing is almost a universal pattern among high-powered researchers. This is not to say that we should stop scientific research. It is to say that the men and women who are doing it *must* be induced to come out of their labs long enough to enter into the public forum and communicate about where we are going and why we are going there. The simple reason for this is that the stakes of what we are doing now are higher than they have ever been before—species survival in terms of the eco-problem and species identity in terms of the biopsychological revolution.

CHOICE

Wisdom is impossible without choice. And choice is impossible without responsibility. Norman Cousins once wrote in a *Saturday Review* editorial that "people involved in a great crisis or upheaval seldom understand what is happening to them." [5] Society is now slowly beginning to realize that we have come through a great upheaval in our physical world as a result of our learning how to generate amazing sources of energy. Every time we turn on a TV we are commanding the electrical energy equivalent of the energy level output of four adult men. Indeed, the availability of almost unlimited amounts of energy at our fingertips has been responsible for moving Western man onto a new threshold of physical existence. But the thing that we don't truly grasp yet is that this conquest of energy also carries with it a mandate to respond psychologically and philosophically to a new kind of world. Unfortunately the major element of our reaction has been to develop an insatiable desire and clamor for more energy—never mind how you rape the land, or exploit others, or what happens when oil is spilled. We are facing a fantastic array of options in terms of our structure and mental being as humans, and no matter how hard we try, it is impossible for us to escape the fact that there are consequences to choice-making. This calls for the emergence of a new kind of responsibility—one that we have really never had before. Developing fingertip energy has been a fantastic revolution; developing a New Man will be even more so.

Man has always resisted change and the so-called movement of history. He has always been psychologically reluctant to accept things such as industrialization and automation. Recently we have added the anxiety that man will lose his identity in a fully computerized and cybernated culture. But we must respond on a level and scale as never before. The problems facing us are ones of human design, and only a new human responsibility will lead to survival and a future. As René Dubos has put it: "We must not ask where science and technology are taking us, but rather how we can manage science and technology so that they can help us get where we want to go." [6] And where we want to go depends on our conception of ourselves.

We can't avoid the responsibility of our choice by saying: But who will make the choice? How can we decide what is best for man? In spite of all our fancy rhetoric about the difficulties of such decisions, there is a blunt reality that all too often gets overlooked. Delgado, the ESB researcher, has stated it clearly and well:

> The fundamental question of who is going to exert the power of behavioral control is easy to answer: everybody who is aware of the elements involved and understands how they act upon us will have that power.[7]

Enough said.

NEW CONSCIOUSNESS

In my view, one of modern man's hang-ups has been a warped hero worship of rationality. The current technological race is basically directed toward doing anything and everything, from creating Teflon-coated toasters for bacon to putting men on the moon. Modern rational man has convinced himself that if a little bit is good, then a lot more must be better. As a result, we have convinced ourselves (at least those who are in power are convinced) that we should accept the spiraling progression from Minuteman to ABM to MIRV to tomorrow's new weapon acronym as a rational endeavor aimed at controlling the warring tendencies of the human species. But this has never worked for man, and we must ask ourselves again what reason is there to think that the balance of terror is any different this time than it was when the bone club replaced the hand as a weapon. Surely what must compel us to change our modern rational approach is the horrible fact that we possess the energy and skill required to destroy ourselves either with the noise of a crescendo of MIRV-ed blows on a city or with the silence of a viral invasion from the countryside. The only way out of this kind of "rationality" is to prepare ourselves to turn from the risk of war to the risk of peace. And to do this, we must tune our rationality into our "feelings."

Charles Reich, in his loudly proclaimed and loudly denounced book *The Greening of America,* has captured in simple but compelling fashion the essence of a new consciousness (called Consciousness III) that he feels is growing in our midst. This book has to be read to believe it, and even then not all who do read it will believe it. It is impossible to review his entire argument without spending a great deal of time, so I shall instead attempt to capture its spirit by culling out a few central and provocative statements.

> Today's emerging consciousness seeks a new knowledge of what it means to be human. . . .[8]

> Rationality does not like to blow its mind. . . . To "blow one's mind" means to become more aware.[9]

The new Consciousness III does not:

> propose to abolish work, or excellence, it proposes to abolish irrational and involuntary servitude. It does not propose to abolish law, organization, or government, it asks instead that they serve rational, human ends.[10]

What's so different about this? That's what all good Americans have always been for—like apple pie and Mother's Day. If that has been your mental response, then you don't yet know what Consciousness III is all about. This kind of consciousness goes on to take a good hard look at the world and concludes: "The discrepancy between what could be and what is, is overwhelming." [11]

Wait, you say again; it's always been that way. Heavens, what's new about an imperfect society? Again, if that is your response, you won't believe the Consciousness III answer because it is so simple that it has disarmed nearly all the reviewers who have tried to point out Reich's foolishness. The answer is: *All that is necessary to describe the new society is to describe a new way of life.* [12]

Not a profound or new thought, but if this kind of revolutionary idea continues to take hold, its power will be "like flowers pushing up through the concrete pavement." [13] Modern man has created a new physical world run by energy, but he has not yet created a consciousness to go along with it. If he creates the New Man, an even newer consciousness will be necessary.

I have a poster over my desk which pictures a small boy bending over and pointing to a flower in a garden. The words describing the scene are simple but compelling:

> Stand still
> and look until
> you really
> see.

This expresses a true need of our world. In our rational rush to generate new knowledge we have forgotten to stop long enough to look at what we are really doing to ourselves. I sometimes wonder what will happen when all our instant products and services are packaged into one single "instant" (for example, instant pudding, instant success by smoking the right cigar, instant sex by using the right soap or underarm deodorant, etc.). What will we do with the rest of our time when all this is crammed into that one blissful instant? The message of this poster is to stop and look. Take time to "feel" what is happening. Ask yourself whether what you see is really what you think it ought to be. If it is not, says Consciousness III, "blow your mind" and change your life. It could be man you are saving.

MAN-IN-RELATION

So far we have talked about wisdom, choice, and a new consciousness. Each of these requires a response at the individual level, since no one else can respond for another person. But that is not the end of it. There is one more crucial point. We are individuals, but we are not separate units unto ourselves. To describe this last linking element in our framework of response to the potentialities of a New Man, I would like to turn again to the place where we began this chapter, Hermann Hesse and his book *Siddhartha*.

Siddhartha, the son of an Indian Brahmin, spends his entire life in a search for the ultimate answer to the significance of man's role on this earth. After a lifetime of searching he finds himself in a suicidal despair by a river he once crossed as a young man. Watching the river rekindles his spark for life and as he approaches a ferryman at the river's edge, Siddhartha asks the most significant question that an individual can ever ask of another: Will you take me across?

Hard as we search, hard as we work, hard as we contemplate the significance of existence and life, eventually we face the realization and truth that we cannot do it alone. As much as we desire wisdom, as much as we yearn for responsible choice, as much as we strive for a new consciousness, we must ask others to "take us across." It is man-in-relation that counts—in relationship to himself, to his fellowmen, to nature, and to God.

Should we dare to create a New Man, we must not only renew our bonds of wisdom, responsibility, and choice, we must also ask of each other: Will you take me across? Moreover, it is my belief that this kind of reaching toward one another is also represented in the challenge of Jesus when he compellingly but poignantly commands: Follow me. To respond is to live. No man is an island. The self-made man is a myth.

CONCLUSION

By now it must be clear that I am convinced that we are standing on a new threshold of challenge which will redefine what it means to be a man or a woman. But this is really nothing new. It has always been this way—man flowing into a future that continually creates new possibilities. We must always put great energy into renewed debates on ancient questions. What is man that thou art mindful of him? What is the meaning of existence? What does it mean to be a man in relation to other men and to God? What is the meaning of responsibility? And perhaps the most exciting question of all: Is man now the creature that he was intended to be?

Yet, in our excitement we must move carefully and slowly, for there is a very serious question to be confronted. It was put this way by the German theologian Helmut Thielicke: "Is there something about man that dare not be changed—something in his very nature that dare not be violated—if he is to remain human?" [14] Man has been in his infancy for the past few thousand years of his development. Change has always been with us, but now we find the knowledge before us to control our destiny—to say what man is to be, rather than to continue as he is or was.

Nobel laureate and geneticist of the first rank, H. J. Muller has expressed the challenge of this power and responsibility in the following fashion:

> Thus we should not let ourselves be discouraged by the temporary difficulties. We should not only bear in mind the urgent need for success. We should also recall that, after all, man has gone from height to height, and that he is now in a position, if only he *will*, to transcend himself intentionally and thereby proceed to elevations yet unimagined. He no longer can do so unintentionally. It is up to us to do our bit in this purposive process, and to use what we know constructively, rather than remain in that ivory tower which has the writing on the wall. Our reward will be that of helping man to gain the highest freedom possible: the finding of endless worlds both outside and inside himself, and the privilege of engaging in endless creation. [15]

What greater challenge is there for man than "engaging in endless creation"?

I shall close with a series of sentences from the essay *Building the Earth*, by Teilhard de Chardin, which focuses on the challenge of the future.

There is now incontrovertible evidence that mankind has just entered upon the greatest period of change the world has ever known. . . . No matter what reactions we may have to current events, we ought first to reaffirm a robust faith in the destiny of man. . . . Today's critical events make a turning-point as well as a crisis in our understanding of progress. . . . This is the crisis of birth, however, not the signs of death. . . . The task before us now, if we would not perish, is to shake off our ancient prejudices, and to build the earth.[16]

It is always the same, and yet every moment it is new. On our way to the future, science is changing the rules of the game. There will be a new world in the morning. But this is a crisis of birth, not death. The future is waiting to be born. Will man lose his nerve or rise to new heights of manhood and womanhood? The next move is ours—together.

Shalom and Agape

P.S. Hang on to Your Hat

If what we have discussed under the headings of mood drugs, ESB, and new methods of reproduction has seemed to be "outta sight," then hang on to your hat, we haven't seen anything yet. To save space and mind we will mention only four prospects in general detail, but they should be enough to convince you that the flow of new possibilities is not going to stop. Remember that possibilities do not always pan out as realities. At the same time, though, they often lead to completely surprising and unpredictable happenings. We will just have to wait and see.

SUPERMOTHERHOOD

According to the *Guinness Book of World Records,* the most children ever born to one woman is sixty-nine (four sets of quadruplets, seven sets of triplets, and sixteen sets of twins).[1] The human ovary has the potential of developing around a half million eggs, but in normal situations, "monthly" ovulation produces only five hundred or so during a woman's fertile lifetime. Hence the record of sixty-nine children is really a drop in the bucket compared to the potential that is there. By a variety of techniques, such as ovary tissue culturing or chemical ripening and releasing of eggs, it is becoming possible to obtain large numbers of eggs at one time. This process of "superovulation" has placed us on the threshold of being able to tap a very large segment of the entire egg potential of one woman.

Work is also proceeding toward developing an artificial placenta which will provide nourishment for an embryo while it grows and develops outside of a natural womb. Since sperm is readily available in any quantity desired, the additional linkages of superovulation with an artificial placenta would be the marriage of technology necessary to bring the assembly-line decanting of offspring in Huxley's Brave New World into reality. Maybe it will be right in time to create the second wave of the population explosion.

Transplants

Kidney and heart transplants now receive only routine attention in the press. To be sure, the rejection problems have not been completely solved, but almost everyone assumes that it is just a matter of time until they are. What about tomorrow? If you can name the organ, chances are that someone is seriously working on transplanting it right now. Two examples will illustrate. Dr. James Scott and his colleagues at the University of Iowa are exploring the possibility of transplanting a nonvital organ, in this case the uterus and Fallopian tubes of female rhesus monkeys.[2] The reproductive glands, the ovary and testes, are also objects of this kind of research. The second example concerns what many feel to be the ultimate in this area—a brain transplant (or a body transplant for those who are turned off by the first expression). We are certainly not on the verge of perfecting this technique to transplant completely functioning brains; however, Dr. Robert White has demonstrated that it is possible to separate the brain of a rhesus monkey from the body and by using blood from another live donor monkey, keep that isolated brain functioning in regard to electrical activity for hours.[3] Quite possibly the technical difficulties of being able to hook up all the nerves and blood vessels to a "host" body so that the brain is returned to a "normal" stage will not be overcome for decades. But we have started down that road.

Transplants can be accomplished with artificial organs as well as living ones. Consider the current level of such transplants in the United States: 40,000 persons have electronic pacemakers to keep their hearts beating and pumping properly; 45,000 have one or more artificial heart valves; tens of thousands have artificial joints in hips, fingers, wrists, etc.; and about 100,000 have sections of artificial arteries. Experiments are well under way to develop artificial kidneys, hearts, livers, and even eyes. Dr. Vincent L. Gott, a leading cardiac surgeon, has summarized the potential of this area: "Eventually, it should be possible to replace more than half of the human body with artificial organs." [4] Psychological crises and identity problems have resulted in transplant recipients, particularly in the case of hearts. So the question is: Who will "transplanted" man be? (Never mind whether it's artificial or real.)

Man's imagination often runs ahead of his ability, and the book *To Live Again,* by Robert Silverberg, is an example of what science fiction buffs are reading today.[5] The story centers around "persona" transplants carried out by a process that allows for storing on tape the entire mind, soul, and experience of any individual. After death, the information on this tape can be transplanted into the brain of another living person to provide a "multi-personality." Having two, three, or more complete personalities inside of one head leads to new heights of creativity as well as to new depths of human agony. Science fiction today. Tomorrow?

Conscious Control of Brain Activity

Outer space has received much attention in the past decade. But recently there have been some startling and revolutionary developments occurring in the "inner space" of the mind world (aside from ESB). Century-old traditions about the inability of man to control voluntarily certain functions of his brain and body have been brought into serious question. The major thrust of these new ideas seems to be along the lines of conscious control over brain activity and certain internal states and body functions.

As we saw earlier, the brain generates electrical patterns of activity. One type of output is called alpha waves, and it has been found that some people can learn to turn this activity on or off at will. In general terms, then, it is possible to learn to recognize and control certain states of brain activity.[6] There are enough questions and implications raised here to keep us busy for a long time, but the central issue centers around what effect learning to control brain rhythms or activity will have on mood, meditation, creativity, and learning ability. It is early in the game, but some researchers have made provocative suggestions; for example, it might be possible to reduce drastically the need for sleep by learning how to stay in the alpha state.

The second general thrust is along the lines of controlling internal states and body functions such as blood pressure, heart rate, respiration, body temperature, and muscular relaxation, all activities heretofore thought to be only under automatic control and beyond significant conscious control.[7] Being able to control one's heart activity by mental discipline alone would surely have an enormous impact on health. Experiments with rats indicate that heart rate training can affect learning and emotional states. The upshot of all this is that it may be possible to counter stress and anxiety by mental effort rather than "popping a pill." In addition, who knows what new states of mental activity might be uncovered in this exploration of inner space?

THE MARRIAGE OF BIOLOGY,
CHEMISTRY,
AND RELIGION

The religious side of man has not been without its attention. Would you believe biochemical theology? This is presented with some feeling of tongue in cheek, but we must recognize that someday we might have to pull our tongue in quickly. Francis Crick, Nobel Prize winner for the co-discovery of DNA structure, speaks for himself:

I therefore feel an obligation to suggest a new subject in which practically no work has been done at all, and I would propose for your consideration biochemical theology. It is not quite true that nobody has researched into such matters as the efficacy of prayer. In the last century, for example, Galton wrote an amusing paper on the subject (Statistical Enquiries into the Efficacy of Prayer) in which he showed by a couple of ingenious statistical tests that the efficacy of prayer seemed to be rather low. This line of work does not appear to have been followed up either by the Church of England or by the Vatican. But nobody, as far as I know, has considered the problem at the biochemical level. So many people pray that one finds it difficult to believe that they do not get some satisfaction from it, and a good molecular biologist will naturally believe that this can be expressed, at least in part, in molecular terms. Part of it, of course, would involve the molecular biology of the synapse and the overall organization of the nervous system, but the principal effect is probably hormonal, and one would not be surprised to find that hormone levels were affected by prayer. No doubt before long some "with-it" church in America will take up the topic.[8]

I can hear the pews rattling now!

Bibliography

There are many more bases in the areas of mood drugs, ESB, and reproduction than have been touched in this book. Indeed, there are numerous untouched bases in many other areas of knowledge that have the same kind of "man-shaking" potential. The books listed below are suggestions of places to go in order to probe deeper and wider into these subjects. They have been chosen because of their readability and ability to provoke new ideas. Most of them have extensive bibliographies that will lead to other general material as well as to the more technical scientific literature.

Mood Drugs

Gamage, James R., and Zerkin, Edmund L. (eds.), *Hallucinogenic Drug Research: Impact on Science and Society*. STASH Press, 1970. Paper.
This book is the proceedings of the First Annual Symposium of the Student Association for the Study of Hallucinogens held at Beloit College in October, 1969. The nine authors are all leading researchers in the drug field, and although the book is now a few years old, it repre-

sents a good survey of the fundamental information in the LSD area.

(NOTE: STASH, the Student Association for Study of Hallucinogens, is a student-run organization directed toward obtaining and disseminating valid information about the psychoactive, or mood-altering, drugs. Information can be obtained by writing STASH, 638 Pleasant Street, Beloit, Wis. 53511.)

Kaplan, John, *Marijuana—The New Prohibition*. The World Publishing Company, 1970; paperback, Pocket Books, Inc.

John Kaplan was one of a group of six lawyers drafted by the California legislature in 1966 to examine and recommend change in that state's criminal laws. Their report on marijuana, however, so infuriated the Legislative Committee that the entire group was fired. This book is the report of the information that led to the author's position that there should be some type of licensing system for marijuana. The information level of the book is high, so each reader can make up his own mind.

Louria, Donald B., *Overcoming Drugs*. McGraw-Hill Book Company, Inc., 1971.

Overcoming Drugs is the sequel to Dr. Louria's highly successful book *The Drug Scene* written in 1968. In addition to a large question and answer section, rather specific proposals are made concerning approaches to young people, parents, education, and legislation.

ESB AND THE BRAIN

Calder, Nigel, *The Mind of Man*. The Viking Press, 1971.

As a result of visits to researchers in eight countries during 1970, this highly respected reporter has put together a wide-ranging survey of "current research on the brain and human nature." The many illustrations are a significant addition to a well-written book.

Delgado, José M. R., *Physical Control of the Mind: Toward a Psychocivilized Society*. Harper & Row, Publishers, Inc., 1969. Cloth and paper.

This is *the* book on ESB. Written by one of the leading researchers in the field, the contents range from the evolution of mental activities, a discussion of mind and soul, experimental control of brain functioning in behaving subjects (animal and human), the ethics of electrical control of the brain, to a plea for the development of a "psychocivilized society." A penetrating and provocative book.

Mark, Vernon H., and Ervin, Frank R., *Violence and the Brain*. Harper & Row, Publishers, Inc., 1970. Cloth and paper.

The theme of this book is that we are overdue for a "new and more rational approach to problems of human violence" which is based on direct treatment of brain dysfunction with ESB-guided surgery. Mark, a neurosurgeon, and Ervin, a psychiatrist, work together in this field. The illustrations are excellent and show how it is done!

Taylor, John, *The Shape of Minds to Come*. Weybright & Talley, Inc., 1971.

Taylor, an author and physicist in England, explores the effects of drugs, hypnosis, telepathy, clairvoyance, and ESB in terms of their future impact on our lives. He argues that free will is an illusion and that organized religion is the institution most responsible for man's "present terrible situation." Guaranteed to provoke a reaction!

NEW METHODS OF REPRODUCTION

Francoeur, Robert T., *Utopian Motherhood: New Trends in Human Reproduction*. Doubleday & Company, Inc., 1970.

A must for the Women's Liberation Movement. Anyone who reads this book will surely be impressed with the fantastic knowledge being gained which will allow us to monitor, guide, and alter every step in the process of human reproduction. In addition to providing clear descriptions of the science involved, Francoeur also deals with the problem of "how these technological innovations have modified man's past view of sexuality and of woman" and how they will change them in the future.

Ramsey, Paul, *Fabricated Man: The Ethics of Genetic Control*. Yale University Press, 1970. Paper.

Paul Ramsey is a scholar trained in the field of ethics who has turned his attention recently to the ethical implications of modern research in genetics and reproduction. One of his key concerns is the balance between maintaining man's freedom and responsibility as opposed to the possibility of species suicide through utilization of schemes for self-modification. In examining the mixed blessings of new knowledge about reproduction, he weaves together his position that we should choose only those options which are "worthy" of man and avoid trying to play God before we have learned to be man.

GENERAL

Augenstein, Leroy, *Come, Let Us Play God*. Harper & Row, Publishers, Inc., 1969.

The most provocative aspect of Augenstein's book is the presentation of actual situations in which decisions had to be made concerning kidney transplants, the use of kidney machines, and abortion. The story of the "third" mongoloid child startles us out of our complacency about dealing with this new knowledge. Many critical questions are raised for discussion. The author does present his answer to the dilemma of deciding in a way that is clear and concise.

London, Perry, *Behavior Control*. Harper & Row, Publishers, Inc., 1969. Cloth and paper.

The impact of this book can be summed up by the following quotation: "As 1984 draws near, it appears that George Orwell's fears for Western democracy may have been too pessimistic, or at least premature, but it is also clear that his concepts of the technology by which tyranny could impress its will upon men's minds were much too modest. By that time, the means at hand will be more sophisticated and efficient than Orwell ever dreamed, and they will be in at least modest use, as they have already begun to be, not by the will of tyrants but by the invitation of all of us, for we have been schooled to readiness for all these things and will demand their benign use regardless of their potential risk."

Rosenfeld, Albert, *The Second Genesis: The Coming Control of Life*. Prentice-Hall, Inc., 1969.

This book is quite similar to *The Biological Time Bomb*. Rosenfeld "shows how man has already entered into a science fiction world of artificial breeding, psychochemicals and cybernetics—a whole new bio-technological environment that will have an overwhelming imprint on the very fundamentals of religion, philosophy, law, sex, morality, and the conduct of our daily lives."

Taylor, Gordon, *The Biological Time Bomb*. The World Publishing Company, 1968; paperback, New American Library, 1969.

This is the book that really kicked off the public awareness of the new biology (as a Book-of-the-Month Club selection). The subjects range as follows: choice of sex in children, organ transplants, immortality, genetic warfare, and creation of life. Taylor's thesis is that the "biological bomb" is "going to explode not in some safe, distant future, but in the lifetime of many now living."

Toffler, Alvin, *Future Shock*. Random House, Inc., 1970. Cloth and paper.

Rather than shrink in fear from the future, Toffler argues that we should instead look the future in the face and "reach out and humanize distant tomorrows." The scope of ideas and topics in this book is impressive. Future Shock is defined as a new social disease in which the rapidity and avalanche of change descending upon us results in a paralysis of mind and a subsequent inability to cope with it. Toffler offers his answer to this disease in a book that may be destined to be a significant landmark in our response to the future.

And One for the Serious Student

Handler, Philip (ed.), *Biology and the Future of Man*. Oxford University Press, Inc., 1970.

Imagine some two hundred top scientific authorities organized into twenty-one panels with a mandate to bring together in a single volume an appraisal of the "state of the art" in the individual subsystems of biology and a statement of where this knowledge might lead us tomorrow. Result: over 900 pages of basic information much of which is directed toward understanding how our knowledge of living phenomena can benefit humanity. Some of the areas covered are molecular biology (genetics), origin of life, biology of development, biology of behavior, ecology, diversity of life, computers and the life sciences, feeding mankind, medical science, environmental health, and biology and the future of man. Unfortunately, there are two serious drawbacks—no index and no references. Nevertheless, this is an amazing book in terms of its scope and readability.

Notes

PROLOGUE:
TO BUILD THE EARTH

1. Pierre Teilhard de Chardin, *Building the Earth* (Avon Books, 1969), p. 23.
2. *Ibid.,* p. 67.

1. ON OUR WAY TO THE FUTURE,
   SCIENCE IS CHANGING THE RULES
   OF THE GAME

1. Alvin Toffler, *Future Shock* (Random House, Inc., 1970), p. 13.
2. David M. Kiefer, "The Futures Business," *Chemical and Engineering News,* Vol. 47, No. 33 (Aug. 11, 1969), p. 68.
3. John R. Platt, "Life Where Science Flows," speech at American Institute of Planners' Conference, Washington, D.C., Oct. 2, 1967.
4. Robert Theobald, *Dialogue on Technology* (The Bobbs-Merrill Company, Inc., 1967), p. 9.
5. Margaret Mead, *Culture and Commitment* (Doubleday & Company, Inc., 1970), p. 58.
6. See Garrett Hardin, "Everybody's Guilty—The Ecological Dilemma," *California Medicine,* Vol. 113, No. 5 (Nov., 1970), pp. 40–47.
7. Robert A. Heinlein, *The Moon Is a Harsh Mistress*

(Berkley Medallion Paperback, Berkley Publishing Corporation, 1968), p. 241.

8. Paul Ramsey, *Fabricated Man: The Ethics of Genetic Control* (Yale University Press, 1970), pp. 150–151. Quotations are reprinted by permission of Yale University Press.

9. Barry Commoner, "Ecological Problems," *Chemical and Engineering News,* Vol. 48, No. 6 (Feb. 9, 1970), p. 80.

10. Garrett Hardin, "The Tragedy of the Commons," *Science,* Vol. 162, No. 3859 (Dec. 13, 1968), pp. 1243–1248.

11. Pierre Teilhard de Chardin, *The Phenomenon of Man* (Harper & Row, Publishers, Inc., 1961), p. 246.

12. H. G. Wells, *The First Men in the Moon* (Berkley Medallion Paperback, Berkley Publishing Corporation, 1967), p. 77.

13. *Ibid.,* p. 116.

2. MOOD DRUGS

1. *Medicines in the 1990's: A Technological Forecast* (London: Office of Health Economics, Oct., 1969), p. 22.

2. *Journal of the American College Health Association,* Vol. 17, No. 5 (June, 1969).

3. *American Journal of Diseases of Children,* Vol. 118, No. 2 (Aug., 1969).

4. *Journal of the American Medical Association,* Vol. 215, No. 10 (March 8, 1971).

5. *Ibid.,* Vol. 216, No. 1 (April 5, 1971).

6. Richard Alpert, Sidney Cohen, and Lawrence Schiller, *LSD* (The New American Library, 1966), p. 8.

7. *Ibid.*

8. Sidney Cohen, "The Uncanny Power of the Hallucinogens," in *The Drug Takers* (Time-Life Books, 1965), p. 91.

9. Walter N. Pahnke, Albert A. Kurland, Sanford Unger, Charles Savage, and Stanislav Grof, "The Experimental Use of Psychedelic (LSD) Psychotherapy," *Journal of the American Medical Association,* Vol. 212, No. 11 (June 15, 1970), pp. 1856–1857.

3. WHICH PILL SHALL I TAKE TODAY— THE RED OR THE GREEN?

1. Name withheld, "Possible Beneficial Uses of LSD-25," unpublished paper, Cornell University, 1971.

2. Robert S. DeRopp, *The Master Game* (Delacorte Press Book, The Dial Press, Inc., 1968), p. 21.

3. *Ibid.*

4. *Ibid.,* p. 22.

5. *Ibid.,* p. 43.

6. *Ibid.*

7. Walter N. Pahnke and William A. Richards, "Implications of LSD and Experimental Mysticism," *Journal of Religion and Health,* Vol. 5, No. 3 (1966), p. 195.

8. From a subject in the Harvard Psilocybin Project. See Alpert, Cohen, and Schiller, *LSD,* p. 59.

9. From Alfred Tennyson. See *ibid.*

10. Wayne O. Evans, "The Psychopharmacology of the Normal Human: Trends in Research Strategy," in *Psychopharmacology,* ed. by Daniel A. Efron (U.S. Government Printing Office, Public Health Service Publication No. 1836, 1968), p. 1003.

11. Helen N. Nowlis, *Drugs on the College Campus* (Doubleday & Company, Inc., 1969), p. 76.

12. Fritz Redl in Harold H. Hart (ed.), *Drugs: For and Against* (Hart Publishing Company, Inc., 1970), pp. 131 ff. Copyright 1970, Hart Publishing Co., Inc., New York. Quotations from this work are reprinted by permission of the publisher.

13. Joel Fort, in *ibid.,* p. 150. Used by permission.

14. Kenneth Keniston, "Drug Use and Student Values," NASPA Drug Education Project Background Paper, pp. 9–10. See Nowlis, *op. cit.,* p. 65.

15. Albert Rosenfeld, *The Second Genesis: The Coming Control of Life* (Prentice-Hall, Inc., 1969), pp. 235 ff.

16. Richard Alpert, in Alpert, Cohen, and Schiller, *op. cit.,* p. 93.

17. Sidney Cohen, in *ibid.*, p. 22.

18. William H. McGlothlin and Louis J. West, "The Marihuana Problem: An Overview," *American Journal of Psychiatry*, Vol. 124, No. 3 (Sept., 1968), p. 375.

19. DeRopp, *op. cit.*, p. 23.

20. Donald B. Louria, *The Drug Scene* (McGraw-Hill Book Company, Inc., 1968), p. 116.

21. Max Rafferty, in Hart (ed.), *op. cit.*, p. 36.

22. Bernard Barber, in *ibid.*, pp. 93, 101.

23. Judianne Densen-Gerber, in *ibid.*, pp. 109, 111.

24. Jules Saltman, *Marijuana and Your Child* (Grosset & Dunlap, Inc., 1970), pp. 109–110.

25. Rafferty, in Hart (ed.), *op. cit.*, p. 29.

26. Richard H. Blum and Associates, *Students and Drugs* (Jossey-Bass, Inc., Publishers, 1969), p. 135.

27. Donald B. Louria, *Overcoming Drugs* (McGraw-Hill Book Company, Inc., 1971), p. 114.

28. DeRopp, *op. cit.*, p. 43.

29. Michael Rossman, in Hart (ed.), *op. cit.*, pp. 188, 189, 196.

30. S. I. Hayakawa, "The Quest for Instant Satori," *Human Potential*, Vol. 2, No. 1 (1969), p. 49.

31. Reported as saying of B. T., a twenty-year-old college student, in John Cashman, *The LSD Story* (Fawcett Publications, Inc., 1966), p. 78.

32. Fort, in Hart (ed.), *op. cit.*, p. 152.

33. Seymour Halleck, "The Great Drug Education Hoax," *STASH Capsules*, Vol. 3, No. 1 (April, 1971), p. 1.

34. John Taylor, *The Shape of Minds to Come* (Weybright & Talley, Inc., 1971), p. 229. Copyright © 1971 by John Taylor. Quotations from this work are reprinted by permission of Weybright & Talley, Inc., and David McKay Company, Inc.

35. Rafferty, in Hart (ed.), *op. cit.*, p. 28.

4. Electrical Stimulation
    of the Brain

1. See Dean E. Wooldridge, *The Machinery of the Brain* (McGraw-Hill Book Company, Inc., 1963), p. 167.

2. Wilder Penfield, "Memory Mechanisms," *A.M.A. Archives of Neurology and Psychiatry*, Vol. 67 (1952), p. 179.

3. See José M. R. Delgado, *Physical Control of the Mind: Toward a Psychocivilized Society* (Harper & Row, Publishers, Inc., 1969), pp. 103 ff.

4. *Ibid.*, p. 108.

5. *Ibid.*

6. *Ibid.*, pp. 159 f.

7. James Olds, "Emotional Centres in the Brain," *Science Journal*, Vol. 3, No. 5 (May, 1967), p. 88.

8. See Delgado, *op. cit.*, pp. 166 ff.

9. See James Olds, "Self-Stimulation of the Brain," *Science*, Vol. 127, No. 3294 (Feb. 14, 1958), pp. 315–324, and Delgado, *op. cit.*, pp. 140–142.

10. See Delgado, *op. cit.*, p. 168.

11. *Ibid.*, 166.

12. *Ibid.*, p. 114.

13. See Delgado, *op. cit.*, pp. 143–147, and Robert G. Heath, "Electrical Self-Stimulation of the Brain in Man," *American Journal of Psychiatry*, Vol. 120, No. 6 (Dec., 1963), pp. 571–577.

14. See Vernon H. Mark and Frank R. Ervin, *Violence and the Brain* (Harper & Row, Publishers, Inc., 1970), pp. 97–108.

15. See Heath, *loc. cit.*

16. See Mark and Ervin, *op. cit.*, pp. 69–91.

17. *Ibid.*, pp. 70–85.

18. *Ibid.*, p. 85.

19. Delgado, *op. cit.*, pp. 91–96.

20. See "Probing the Brain," *Newsweek*, Vol. 78, No. 4 (July 26, 1971), p. 62.

5. PLUGGED-IN BEHAVIOR

1. Mark and Ervin, *op. cit.*
2. *Ibid.,* p. 14.
3. *Ibid.,* p. 37.
4. *Ibid.*
5. *Ibid.,* p. 47.
6. *Ibid.,* p. 147.
7. *Ibid.,* p. 148.
8. Wooldridge, *op. cit.,* p. 112.
9. Delgado, *op. cit.,* p. 12
10. Delgado as quoted in Maggie Scarf, "Brain Researcher José Delgado Asks—'What Kind of Humans Would We Like to Construct?'" *The New York Times Magazine,* Nov. 15, 1970, p. 46.
11. Delgado as quoted in Scarf, *ibid.,* p. 154.
12. Delgado, *op. cit.,* p. 259.
13. Taylor, *op. cit.,* pp. 25–26.
14. Perry London, *Behavior Control* (Harper & Row, Publishers, Inc., 1969), pp. 149–150.
15. Rosenfeld, *op. cit.,* p. 56.
16. Delgado as quoted in Scarf, *op. cit.,* p. 166.
17. Taylor, *op. cit.,* p. 35.
18. *Ibid.,* p. 231.
19. *Ibid.,* p. 49.
20. Rosenfeld, *op. cit.,* pp. 219–220.
21. Delgado, *op. cit.,* pp. 222–223.
22. *Ibid.,* p. 249.
23. Morton Reiser as quoted in Scarf, *op. cit.,* p. 172.
24. London, *op. cit.,* p. 151.
25. Taylor, *op. cit.,* p. 230.
26. Rosenfeld, *op. cit.,* p. 273.
27. Taylor, *op. cit.,* p. 237.

6. Sex and the Single Cell

1. Robert T. Francoeur, *Utopian Motherhood: New Trends in Human Reproduction* (Doubleday & Company, Inc., 1970), pp. vii–viii.
2. James D. Watson, "Potential Consequences of Experimentation with Human Eggs," presented to Panel on Science and Technology, 12th meeting, Committee on Science and Astronautics, U.S. House of Representatives, 92d Congress, 1st Session, Jan. 26–28, 1971, p. 158.

7. The Birds and Bees Revisited

1. Rollo May, *Love and Will* (W. W. Norton & Company, Inc., 1969), p. 311.
2. *Ibid.*
3. *Ibid.*
4. *Ibid.*
5. *Ibid.*
6. Aldous Huxley, *Brave New World* (Doubleday & Company, Inc., 1932), p. 15.
7. Ramsey, *op. cit.*, pp. 122–123.
8. *Ibid.*, p. 123.
9. Joshua Lederberg, "Genetic Engineering and the Amelioration of Genetic Defect," *BioScience*, Vol. 20, No. 24 (Dec. 18, 1970), p. 1309.
10. Bernard D. Davis, "Prospects for Genetic Intervention in Man," *Science*, Vol. 170, No. 3964 (Dec. 18, 1970), p. 1282.
11. Ramsey, *op. cit.*, p. 88. Quotations from this source, identified in notes 11, 12, 15, 17, and 21, appeared first in Kenneth Vaux (ed.), *Who Shall Live? Medicine, Technology, Ethics* (Fortress Press, 1970).
12. *Ibid.*, pp. 88–89.
13. Francoeur, *op. cit.*, p. 49.
14. Harold Kuhn, "The Prospect of Carbon-Copy Humans," *Christianity Today*, Vol. 25, No. 14 (April 9, 1971), p. 642.
15. Ramsey, *op. cit.*, p. 78.

16. Joshua Lederberg, "Experimental Genetics and Human Evolution," *The American Naturalist,* Vol. 100, No. 915 (Sept.–Oct., 1966), p. 531.

17. Attributed to Lederberg, in Ramsey, *op. cit.,* p. 73.

18. Davis, *op. cit.,* p. 1281.

19. Francoeur, *op. cit.,* p. 156.

20. James D. Watson, "Moving Toward the Clonal Man," *Atlantic,* Vol. 227, No. 11 (May, 1971), p. 52.

21. Ramsey, *op. cit.,* p. 95.

22. Watson, *op. cit.,* p. 53.

23. Francoeur, *op. cit.,* p. 157

8. A NEW WORLD
IN THE MORNING

1. Hermann Hesse, *Siddhartha* (A New Directions Paperback, 1951), p. 83.

2. See E. N. da C. Andrade, *Sir Isaac Newton* (Doubleday & Company, Inc., n.d.), p. 134.

3. John R. Platt, *The Excitement of Science* (Houghton Mifflin Company, 1962), pp. 61–62.

4. See James K. Blasman, "Harvard Genetics Researcher Quits Science for Politics," *Science,* Vol. 167, No. 3920 (Feb. 13, 1970), p. 963.

5. Norman Cousins, in *Saturday Review,* Vol. 52, No. 17 (April 26, 1969), p. 26.

6. As reported by Archibald MacLeish, "The Great American Frustration," *Saturday Review,* Vol. 51, No. 28 (July 13, 1968), p. 16.

7. Delgado, *op. cit.,* p. 256.

8. Charles Reich, *The Greening of America* (Random House, Inc., 1970), p. 5.

9. *Ibid.,* pp. 100, 254.

10. *Ibid.,* p. 356.

11. *Ibid.,* p. 220.

12. *Ibid.,* p. 357.

13. *Ibid.,* p. 395.

14. Helmut Thielicke, "The Doctor as Judge of Who Shall

Live and Who Shall Die," in Kenneth Vaux (ed.), *Who Shall Live?* (Fortress Press, 1970), p. 146.

15. H. J. Muller, "What Genetic Course Will Man Steer?" *Bulletin of the Atomic Scientists,* Vol. 24, No. 3 (March, 1968), p. 12.

16. Teilhard de Chardin, *Building the Earth,* pp. 49, 51, 54, 67.

P.S. HANG ON TO YOUR HAT

1. Norris and Ross McWhirter (eds.), *Guinness Book of World Records* (10th ed., Bantam Books, Inc., 1971), p. 23.

2. *Science News,* Vol. 100, No. 1 (July 3, 1971), p. 11.

3. Oriana Fallaci, "The Dead Body and the Living Brain," *Look,* Vol. 31, No. 24 (Nov. 28, 1969), pp. 99 ff.

4. Howard J. Sanders, "Artificial Organs," *Chemical and Engineering News,* Vol. 49, No. 14 (April 5, 1971), p. 35.

5. Robert Silverberg, *To Live Again* (Doubleday & Company, Inc., 1969).

6. See David M. Rorvik, "The Wave of the Future—Brain Waves," *Look,* Vol. 34, No. 20 (Oct. 6, 1970), pp. 88 ff., and Bernard Law Collier, "Brain Power: The Case for Bio-Feedback Training," *Saturday Review,* Vol. 54, No. 15 (April 10, 1971), pp. 10 ff.

7. Harold M. Schmeck, Jr., "Control by Brain Studied as Way to Curb Body Ills," *The New York Times,* Jan. 9, 1971, pp. 1 ff.

8. Francis Crick, "Molecular Biology in the Year 2000," *Nature,* Vol. 228, No. 5272 (Nov. 14, 1970), p. 615.